ENDORSEMENTS

My dear friend, Dr. Michael Maiden, has written a wonderful new book, *What Is Heaven Saying?* This book is brilliant. Simply brilliant. I have benefited profoundly through the years from his amazing ability to hear from God and proclaim over my life what he heard Him say. And I will never be the same. I'm thrilled that this seasoned prophet has made his insight known to the rest of us in this book. For while not all are prophets, all may prophesy. Perhaps it would be better said, all must prophesy! Here the author lays out the practical approach to hearing from God and speaking what is on His heart. Dr. Maiden wisely includes the pitfalls and challenges that come along with this gift. But instead of being a people who avoid the prophetic because of its dangers, we must become a people who together learn to embrace this gift because of its potential fruit and impact. If we stay humble and biblically based, we can learn the beauty of taking the risks necessary to bring strength and insight to those around us. Our world desperately needs believers to pursue God's voice, releasing His divine destiny and clarity to our world. Please read this empowering book, and be forever changed.

BILL JOHNSON
Senior Leader of Bethel Church, Redding, CA
Author of *The Way of Life* and *Born for Significance*

Dr. Michael Maiden's new book, *What Is Heaven Saying?* isn't simply a handbook on how to operate in the gift of prophecy. Rather, it's written by one who has taken up residence in God's heart and has become a master teacher of bridging the spiritual chasm often found between people's hearts and minds. This book eliminates spiritual distance, clarifies any potential confusion around the gift of prophecy, and restores the Word of God back into the mouths of those who believe.

To quote Dr. Maiden, "...prophecy is not restricted to a few people with a prophetic gift. If you are a born-again believer, you are supposed to prophesy, too!" It's with great pleasure that I recommend this book to any Believer who desires more than just a spiritual gift but also the gift of truly knowing the voice of our Almighty God.

KRIS VALLOTTON
Leader, Bethel Church, Redding, CA
Co-Founder of Bethel School of
Supernatural Ministry
Author of twelve books, including
The Supernatural Ways of Royalty, Heavy Rain and *Poverty, Riches and Wealth*

It is not often you come across someone who literally brings God to you in such a way that is undeniable and life changing. Michael Maiden is such a person. His prophetic accuracy, combined with his genuine and humility of spirit is without a doubt having a global impact. His book *What Is Heaven Saying?*, carries insight and should become a must for every Kingdom leader and believer who desires to carry a prophetic edge. Thank you, Dr. Michael, for releasing your insight into such an important area. *What Is Heaven Saying?*, will help you to discover how to unlock supernatural doors and release Gods purpose both in life and leadership.

PAUL DE JONG
Senior Leader of LIFE, New Zealand

Michael Maiden, without a doubt, can best be described as one of the most legitimate prophetic voices in the kingdom. There is a fine line between the prophetic and the pathetic. Dr. Maiden's exercise of this Spirit-empowered gift legitimizes for an entire generation the undeniable fact that God speaks to us today in a very personal and direct matter. Must read, must do, must live out!

SAMUEL RODRIGUEZ
New Season Lead Pastor
NHCLC President
Author of *You Are Next!*
Executive Producer of the movie, Breakthrough

In a time of chaos and confusion we need to hear what Heaven is saying about our lives and situations. Dr. Maiden has written a must-read book for those that are longing for a supernatural perspective rather than the normal perspective. I recommend this book highly to everyone longing to hear from God.

BENNY PEREZ
Lead Pastor
ChurchLV

WHAT is HEAVEN SAYING?

YOUR HANDBOOK TO OPERATING IN THE GIFT OF PROPHECY

MICHAEL MAIDEN

DESTINY IMAGE® PUBLISHERS, INC.

P.O. Box 310, Shippensburg, PA 17257-0310

"Promoting Inspired Lives."

This book and all other Destiny Image and Destiny Image Fiction books are available at Christian bookstores and distributors worldwide.

Cover design by Eileen Rockwell
Interior design by Terry Clifton

For more information on foreign distributors, call 717-532-3040.

Reach us on the Internet: www.destinyimage.com.

ISBN 13 TP: 978-0-7684-5341-6
ISBN 13 eBook: 978-0-7684-5342-3
ISBN 13 HC: 978-0-7684-5344-7
ISBN 13 LP: 978-0-7684-5343-0

For Worldwide Distribution, Printed in the U.S.A.

2 3 4 5 6 7 8 / 24 23 22 21 20

CONTENTS

Chapter 1

OPEN THE DOOR TO
THE SUPERNATURAL

M ost Christians believe that we are approaching the end of "the last days" and God is moving in our world at an accelerated pace. You are called to play a special prophetic part in this great "move of God." Yet, we have to be careful not to adopt a negative view of the world and believe that everything is bad and getting worse. Everything ain't bad in the Kingdom!

In fact, there are more Christians alive today on the planet than have existed throughout the ages since the crucifixion. We are living in the greatest worldwide move of God creation has ever seen and most Christians are unaware of it.

The following are a few examples: up to 30 percent of China has become Christian, Communism can't keep Christ out of China; up to 35 percent of Indonesia, the largest Muslim nation in the world, has come to Christ— Islam can't keep Christ out of Indonesia.

We need to keep tuned to the message of Heaven because it is broadcasting a different message than we are hearing on the news. If we are not careful, we will mistakenly judge our world by the negative circumstances of our lives or the problems of our country. However, to be relevant and take our prophetic place in what God is doing in our day, it is important to be knowledgeable about both worlds.

We are nearing the end of the age but there are many things God must do before the end comes and you have an important and, yes, prophetic part to play.

THE MODERN UN-PROPHETIC CHURCH

The focus of the Christian church as a whole in the United States has descended into the realms of logic and reason and has become, almost exclusively, a teaching-based environment. We have convinced Christians that they need to come to church to learn how to become better persons and be more successful in life.

Although there is an element of truth in that belief, the cost of intellectualizing the church has been the loss of the moving of God's Spirit in our midst. God, however, wants to reclaim His church and return it to His original intention. He wants it to be more than a place where you hear about God, how to live godly lives, and get your spiritual "fix" for the week. He wants it to again become a place where you actually meet with Him.

The time is coming when pastors of "seeker-friendly churches" will come to Spirit-filled churches that haven't compromised and cry out, "We want what you have. Although we have experienced a kind of success, it is not what we had hoped it would be. We want and desperately need more!"

There is a deep longing in every individual for *more,* and a major part of that more is the supernatural. When the church withholds the supernatural, all kinds of negative things happen. The longing for the supernatural takes people into the world of psychics, spiritualists, New Age practices, and other supernatural manifestations from the enemy. We long for the supernatural because we are supernatural people. We are spirit beings as well as physical ones.

Being born again is supernatural. Being baptized in the Spirit and speaking in a heavenly tongue is supernatural. Actually, everything about our walk with God is supernatural.

ELDAD, MEDAD, AND YOU (DAD?)

The eleventh chapter of the book of Numbers tells the story of a strange thing that happened. God had Moses appoint seventy elders to help bear the responsibility for the leadership of the Israelites and He promised to place some of the Holy Spirit that rested on Moses upon them. When the elders came together at the tabernacle to receive their impartation, the Spirit came upon them with the evidence that they began to prophesy.

Then the "strangest thing" happened, two other men who were not elders or in any way special and were not even in the vicinity of the tabernacle also began to prophesy. Their names were Eldad and Medad. When news of this came to Joshua, he suggested to Moses that he should make them stop prophesying.

It didn't seem right to Joshua for them to prophesy because they were not special in any way. They weren't elders or spiritual leaders, just ordinary people. We would say they weren't pastors, teachers, evangelists, or apostles and they certainly were not prophets, just ordinary members of the congregation.

Moses replied to Joshua in a way that surprised him and might surprise you, too: *"But Moses replied, 'Are you jealous for my sake? I wish that all the Lord's people were prophets and that the Lord would put his Spirit upon them all!'"* (Numbers 11:29 NLT).

As a believer, you too have the right to walk with God in the fellowship of revelation. Remember what Jesus said in John 10:27, *"My sheep hear My voice...."* Prophecy is merely speaking aloud what the Shepherd is saying to you.

THE "ALL FLESH" PROMISE

In Acts 1:8, Jesus told the disciples that He had to leave them, but promised that He would send them the Holy Spirit who would be everything He had been and much more. He told them that the coming of the Holy Spirit would empower them and make it possible for them to be witnesses of Him throughout the earth.

The Holy Spirit's arrival on the planet was on the feast Day of Pentecost when the 120 believers in Christ were together in the Upper Room. You probably know the story: there was a loud sound like the roaring of a mighty wind and everyone was filled with the Holy Spirit and began speaking in tongues and flames of fire settled upon each of their heads (Acts 2:1-4).

A loud noise was created by the coming of the Holy Spirit and the Holy Spirit baptism of the 120. It was so noisy that a large crowd of curious Jews gathered to find out what was going on. Many of them thought it was just a wild, drunken party. Then Peter stepped up to explain that what they were hearing was not merrymaking but rather a sound created by the fulfillment of a promise made by God hundreds of years earlier (Acts 2:5-15).

Because these were all Jews who had been schooled in the Old Testament, Peter was able to say, "This is that." So, to understand "this," which was the coming of the Holy Spirit, you had to know what "that" was, and "that" was a prophecy made by Joel.

Peter quoted that prophecy and explained:

> *"And it shall come to pass in the last days,"* says God, *"that I will **pour out of My Spirit on all flesh; your sons and your daughters shall prophesy**, your young men shall see visions, your old men shall dream dreams. And on My menservants and on My maidservants I will pour out My Spirit in those days; and **they shall prophesy**"* (Acts 2-17-18).

Did you get it? God said through Joel and again through Peter that everyone who receives the Holy Spirit would prophesy. At the risk of pointing out the obvious, let me emphasize that this Scripture says that prophecy is *not* restricted to a few people with a prophetic gift. It means that if you are a born-again believer, you are supposed to prophesy, too!

THE LAW OF FIRST MENTION

The Law of First Mention simply means that the very first time an important word or concept is mentioned in the Bible, that Scripture gives that word its most complete and accurate meaning. It serves as a key in understanding the biblical concept and also provides a foundation for its fuller development in later parts of the Bible.

This "First Mention" in the New Testament of the arrival of the Holy Spirit explains that a primary purpose and mission of the Holy Spirit is to bring a prophetic mantle to God's people.

The empowerment that came through the gift of prophecy and other supernatural gifts given by the Holy Spirit that day were the means by which the early church would spread the "Good News" of the Kingdom throughout the earth. Things haven't changed! We are supposed to reach our world through exactly the same means.

Joel's promise of prophecy, visions, and dreams are all supernatural manifestations for the purpose of declaring to humankind how much God loves and cares and what He longs to do for them. All three of these supernatural manifestations have the same purpose—to reveal His will to humankind. God was saying in Joel that when His Holy Spirit comes, it would enable *"all flesh"* to move in those supernatural realms.

ARE YOU PART OF GOD'S PROBLEM?

God wants to give everyone on earth words of prophecy; but if those prophecies were letters, we would have to say that He's got more letters in His mail room than He has people to deliver them. So, God is looking for anyone who will deliver His letters of love. He will use anybody; because it is not and has never been about the delivery person, it is all about the letter.

In Amos 3:7 God explains something important concerning His use of prophecy: *"Surely the Lord God does nothing, unless He reveals His secret to His servants the prophets."*

God doesn't do anything unless He reveals it to the prophets. It is important to notice that the word *prophet* is plural in this verse. So, if someone says that God has revealed a secret to them that no one else knows, don't listen to that person. In fact, we ought not to put the full weight of our belief behind any prophetic word until it is confirmed through the prophecy of others.

Amos 3:8 goes on to say, *"A lion has roared! Who will not fear? The Lord God has spoken! Who can but prophesy?"* This Scripture is saying that just as being in the presence of a lion naturally produces fear, prophesying after encountering God's presence should be just as normal. In Revelation 5:5, Jesus is called the *"Lion of...Judah"* and He is roaring a word for every person.

PROPHECY OPENS THE DOOR FOR MINISTRY

Unfortunately there are many pastors who give no credence to the prophetic and consequently are merely teachers and administrators. The problem that creates is they can only bring the people in their church as high as their relationship with God and their understanding of His ways.

There is certainly nothing wrong with teaching God's Word. However, God often uses prophecy to give His Word credence. Look at what happened when Jesus met the Samaritan woman at Jacob's well.

When Jesus talked with her, her prejudice against Jews made her unreachable to Jesus until He spoke to her prophetically. He promised her water that would give eternal life; and when she asked to know more, He suggested she bring her husband so that He could explain it to both of them. She told him that she didn't have a husband and Jesus replied prophetically:

> …*"You have well said, 'I have no husband,' for you have had five husbands, and the one whom you now have is not your husband; in that you spoke truly." The woman said to Him, "Sir, I perceive that You are a prophet"* (John 4:17-19).

Once Jesus spoke prophetically, the woman raced back to the city screaming, *"Come, see a Man who told me all things I ever did."* She brought the entire city out to hear Him and the Bible says that the result was *"many believed"* (John 4:29,39).

If Christ needed prophecy to make His ministry more effective, then how much more should we be using it to successfully bring the truth of eternal life to our world?

YOU'VE BEEN PROMISED A POWERFUL GIFT

In First Corinthians 12:1, Paul says, *"Now concerning spiritual gifts, brethren, I do not want you to be ignorant."* Then Paul talked about the nine spiritual endowments or gifts that God was giving to believers. Remember, Jesus promised "power" to His followers after the Holy Spirit had come upon them (Luke 24:49), and this is the power He was talking about:

> *But the manifestation of the Spirit is given to each one for the profit of all: for to one is given the word of wisdom through the Spirit, to another the word of knowledge through the same Spirit, to another faith by the same Spirit, to another gifts of healings by the same Spirit, to another the working of miracles, to another prophecy, to another discerning of spirits, to another different kinds of tongues, to another the interpretation of tongues* (1 Corinthians 12:7-10).

Later, in First Corinthians 14, Paul refines his teaching concerning the gift of prophecy. In verse 1 he says, *"Pursue love, and desire spiritual gifts, but especially that you may prophesy."*

Anyone who does not *"pursue love"* becomes defiled in prophecy because prophecy that is not grounded in grace and love will always be bent the wrong way and hurt people rather than help them. At best, it will produce a mixed outcome in people's lives.

While preaching in Tucson, Arizona, one day, God showed me that some handsome men located in the third or fourth row were homosexuals. Many who received that kind of information from God would freak out and start casting, loosening, and binding the devil. I wasn't entirely sure what to do with the information, so I stopped preaching and allowed God to prophesy to them through me.

I picked out one of the guys and God showed me three astonishing facts about his life. When I prophetically told him about the first time he was sexually abused, he fell to the floor. He didn't do the charismatic swoon and fall gently backward to be caught and eased down; he dropped straight down like a rock and began shaking. That night he discovered the God who loves him and his life and the lives of the men with him dramatically changed.

The lesson is this: you cannot allow your thinking, attitudes, or opinions to influence your prophetic gift, or your gift will be tainted. If you do so, it will not have the effect that God desires it to have. Prophecy should come out of a river of love, grace, and healing. If any other streams of thought enter that river, prophecy becomes defiled to the extent of its influence.

Between First Corinthians chapter 12, where the gift of prophecy is listed, and chapter 14, where the gift of prophecy is described, is chapter 13, the "love chapter," which tells us:

> *Though I speak with the tongues of men and of angels, but **have not love, I have become sounding brass or a clanging cymbal**. And though I have the gift of prophecy, and understand all mysteries and all knowledge, and though I have all faith, so that I could remove mountains, **but have not love, I am nothing*** (1 Corinthians 13:1-2).

JUST GO FOR IT

Again, First Corinthians 14:1 says, *"Pursue love, and desire spiritual gifts, but especially that you may prophesy."* God is telling us to burn with passion, ardently pursue and desire with zeal the gift of prophecy.

You might think, *Well, if He wants me to prophesy, fine. I'll be happy to do it, but He has never given me that gift. I've never had a word for anyone.* Sorry, but with that attitude you will never prophesy.

No! God is challenging *you* to pursue Him for the gift of prophecy. Every gift of God comes to you only when you pursue Him for it.

God didn't make you become born again or sneak up on you one day and fill you with the Baptism of the Holy Spirit. You have to desire it and seek it before you can experience it! So why would He, out of the blue, drop on you the gift of prophecy? God never operates that way.

THIS GIFT IS IN YOU—PROPHESY!

Paul explained that there are nine gifts of the Holy Spirit—but then he pulls one gift out, prophecy, and makes it primary by contrasting it to speaking in tongues:

> *He who prophesies speaks edification and exhortation and comfort to men. He who speaks in a tongue edifies himself, but he who prophesies edifies the church. I wish you all spoke with tongues, but even more that you prophesied; for he who prophesies is greater than he who speaks with tongues...*
> (1 Corinthians 14:3-5).

Read the first sentence of First Corinthians 14:3 again and you will discover the definition and purpose of prophecy. It is intended for *"edification and exhortation and comfort."* To edify is to improve by enlightening, to exhort is to encourage and to comfort is to give support and relief. If you believe that you have a prophecy from God but it doesn't accomplish those things, then you should not give it.

Believe it or not, prophecy is the gift that can be most commonly expressed through *everyone* and has the most lasting effect for the Church.

Take another look at First Corinthians 14:4-5 (NLT): *"A person who speaks in tongues is strengthened personally, but one who speaks a word of prophecy strengthens the entire church. I wish you could all speak in tongues, but even more I wish you could all prophesy…."*

Did you see that? According to Paul, everyone should speak in tongues to build themselves up and everyone should prophesy to build up others. You might be thinking, *But what would happen if everyone in the church gave a prophecy?* I'm glad you asked because Paul gives the answer in First Corinthians 14:24-25:

> *But if all prophesy, and an unbeliever or an uninformed person comes in, he is convinced by all, he is convicted by all. And thus the secrets of his heart are revealed; and so, falling down on his face, he will worship God and report that God is truly among you.*

My dream is that every time an unsaved or unspiritual person attends a church service that prophecy would propel the person toward God. However, my highest dream is that we would take this gift of the Holy Spirit to the streets. Imagine what we could do.

Just in case you've read this chapter and still have lingering doubts about whether you *should* and whether you *could* prophesy, let's take a look at First Corinthians 14:31, *"For you can all prophesy one by one, that all may learn and all may be encouraged."*

RIDICULOUS PROPHECIES

One stumbling block to prophecy that I want to mention—prophecy is never solely about what is in the past or present, it is also about what God intends for the future. Often prophecy provides the impartation for you to do something for God that is beyond your wildest dreams or your present abilities.

Many years ago a prophet said to me that I was going to be a writer. Hopefully my face didn't show it, but I was laughing inside because I knew that was ridiculous. I had no desire or ability to write. A few days later, I was seeking the Lord for a sermon but nothing was coming. I asked God why He wasn't speaking to me.

He replied, "Why should I speak to you now when you refuse to believe what I told you in the past?" I knew exactly what He was talking about, writing, and

I immediately repented for not receiving the word He had given me and got my sermon. A few days later, God unfolded a truth to me that He enabled me to write into a book.

Just because a prophecy looks ridiculous or sounds impossible does not mean that it is not a valid prophecy.

WHAT SHOULD YOU DO NEXT?

So, my dear brothers and sisters, be eager to prophesy, and don't forbid speaking in tongues (1 Corinthians 14:39 NLT).

- Begin right now to pray and sincerely ask God to activate the gift of prophecy in you.

- If you don't feel any longing to prophesy, ask God to fill you with a burning desire to do so.

- If you feel unworthy of this gift, remind yourself that you weren't worthy of salvation either, but He gave it to you.

- Remember, you are seeking God for a "gift" not a "reward" for how wonderfully spiritual you are. A time is coming when you will receive your *reward*, but now is the time to receive His *gift* of prophecy.

- Take a moment now and ask God for this gift that God's Word declares is available to every Christian.

- If you have a prayer language, begin to pray earnestly in the Spirit.

I speak over you: "Receive, in the name of Jesus, your gift of prophecy!" Now, put away any doubts and fears, accept that you are to prophesy, and ask God to speak through you to help someone today.

Chapter 2

YOUR INVITATION TO THE PROPHETIC

You really can learn to hear God's voice and be used in the prophetic while reading this book *if* you:

- Come to believe that God is speaking to you and that you have the right to hear Him.

- Develop a deep *desire* to hear Him.

- Find the courage to "go for it."

Many people believe they can't hear God speak because they aren't holy enough or important enough. Some believe that only those who operate in one of the fivefold ministry gifts—apostle, prophet, evangelist, pastor, or teacher—are allowed to actually hear God and receive spiritual gifts.

That, my friend, is a lie the devil wants you to believe to keep you from your God-given gifts and the fullness of your destiny.

This is the season for us to say to ourselves and to God, "I want it all. I want it all because Jesus died to give me it all." Imagine how sad it would be to go to Heaven and learn that God had much more to give you than you allowed yourself to receive. Only when we empty out the treasure chest of God's gifts for us can we make Him truly happy. Imagine how you would feel if you offered someone a life-changing gift and the person didn't have enough understanding, interest, or courage to receive it.

You might want to shout aloud to God right now: I WANT IT ALL, ALL THAT YOU DESIRE FOR ME TO HAVE!

IT'S A NEW SEASON, A NEW DAY

Do you remember from your high school days when the "in-crowd" had a party and only the elite were invited? If you're like me, you never got an invitation. However, when God throws a party, He invites everyone, all are welcome—but it wasn't always that way.

In the Old Testament, under the Old Covenant, very few people had a personal connection with God that made it possible to hear His voice. The high priests could connect with God, but only once a year when they entered the Holy of Holies. When people of that day wanted to receive forgiveness from God, they had to take a sacrifice for their sins to the priest who made the offering to God on their behalf. Under the Old Covenant, prophets, for the most part, were the only people who heard from God.

That was because Adam's sin created a chasm that could not be crossed because it separated all human beings from their Maker. Only under very special circumstances could a uniquely anointed person hear God speak. However, when Jesus became the sacrifice for our sins, He bridged the chasm on our behalf and reopened two-way communications.

In the New Covenant, God speaks by His Holy Spirit to every believer:

> *...For you were slaughtered, and your blood has ransomed people for God from every tribe and language and people and nation. And **you have caused them to become a Kingdom of priests** for our God. And they*

will reign on the earth (Revelation 5:9-10 NLT).

Do you see the amazing thing that happened? You are no longer an outsider; as a born-again believer you are now part of the in-crowd and welcomed to the party. You're not only accepted at the party but as a priest of God's Kingdom destined to reign on the earth—you are the reason for the party.

Therefore Paul could say, *"So let us come boldly to the throne of our gracious God. There we will receive his mercy, and we will find grace to help us when we need it most"* (Hebrews 4:16 NLT).

God is not withholding from us any "good thing." So, this is a season for us to go for it and to receive everything God has promised to the citizens of His earthly Kingdom.

WELCOME TO THE PRIESTHOOD

Okay, so what does it mean to be a "priest"? Isn't a priest a person God will listen to and to whom God can speak? Consider for a moment what it means that the Creator of the universe would listen to us and even speak to us. What an incredible honor we've been given and how sad that so few participate in it.

In the Old Covenant, God spoke through angels, prophets, priests, and some specially chosen and highly anointed people including Moses and King David. In those days, only a few were part of the in-crowd with God.

Unfortunately, some have tried to bring the ways of the Old Covenant into the New Covenant, but they don't fit. In the New, there is no middle man between you and God; so we don't need a confessional booth in the back of the church. Because you are a priest, God hears you when you confess your sins directly to Him. Revelation 1:5-6 says:

> *...To Him who loved us and washed us from our sins in His own blood, and **has made us kings** [and queens] **and priests to His God** and Father, to Him be glory and dominion forever and ever. Amen.*

Every believer has access to the throne of the Creator of the universe; in fact, His throne is your "Mercy Seat." To get an answer from God when you have a prayer request, you don't need to come to me or your pastor and ask us to pray. No. If you bring a prayer request to me, we will pray together as people who are equally kings and priests in God's Kingdom.

Our position as believers is stated again in Revelation 5:10: *"And have made us kings and priests to our God; and we shall reign on the earth."*

It is God's will that we in the Church rise up in the last days to reign on the earth and we will do so by the power given to us through the gifts of the Spirit.

AS A KING OR QUEEN, YOU HAVE AUTHORITY

We have been given spiritual authority and dominion over evil. Jesus said, *"Behold, I give you the authority to trample on serpents and scorpions, and over all the power of the enemy, and nothing shall by any means hurt you"* (Luke 10:19). So you can rebuke the enemy, cast him out and bind him.

As kings we have authority; but as priests, we are under authority and bow down before God.

Priests have a legitimate right to hear and be heard by their God, but our relationship with God is even more intimate than that. Romans 8:14 (NLT) tells us, *"For all who are led by the Spirit of God, are children of God."*

Sons and daughters have an inborn right to hear the voice of their father. According to Romans 8:14, we are the spiritual sons and daughters of God and He has given us His Holy Spirit to facilitate our communications. Under the Old Covenant, God spoke to the earth by angels and prophets, but now He speaks to the earth by His Holy Spirit through His sons and daughters— you and me. Do you get it yet? You have an incredible ability; but more than that, a "right" to speak to and hear from your Father and your God.

The devil does not want you to understand your rights and powers as a priest-king believer. He knows better than most of us that if and when we begin to act like sons and daughters and priests and kings, we will be a royal pain in his backside.

Now it makes sense why each of us has the potential to be world shakers and history makers in the part of the world in which we live. Some would call that location our place in the "Mountains of Culture." (For more information about the Mountains of Culture, check out my book, *Turn the World Upside Down*.)

So keep praying, keep declaring, keep worshipping God and pressing in to Him, and just watch what He does for you and through you.

YOU HAVE INVISIBLE ORGANS

Yep, it's true that God has given each and every believer invisible "ears to hear" and "eyes to see." These unseen parts of you are similar to their visible counterparts. "Eyes to see" allow you to gaze into the spirit realm with understanding and "ears to hear" allow you to perceive what God is saying to you through the Holy Spirit.

As you probably know, humans are three-part beings—we live in a body, experience life through our soul, and have a supernatural aspect called our spirit. So, another way of looking at this is, when the spiritual aspect of your being becomes inhabited by the Holy

Spirit at salvation, the eyes and ears of your spirit, once dormant, are opened. That is why the Bible states: *"Or do you not know that your body is the temple of the Holy Spirit who is in you, whom you have from God..."* (1 Corinthians 6:19).

Therefore, as a son or daughter of God who is a Spirit being, you have the capacity to hear what your spiritual Father says to your spirit.

When Jesus spoke to the Seven Churches in the book of Revelation, He preceded each statement with the phrase, *"He who has an ear, let him hear what the Spirit says to the churches..."* (Revelation 2:7). This is another conformation that you *do* have spiritual ears that *can* hear what Jesus says.

DRIVE LIKE A PROPHET

God often speaks to us through the words of Scripture and the nudging of our hearts. You don't always need a prophetic word to receive prophetic direction. The Bible often calls this silent type of communication from God "bearing witness."

The bearing witness method used by the Holy Spirit to direct us can be compared to what we encounter while driving. When you ask for guidance from God, you may encounter a stoplight, a caution sign, a green light, or some other road-like sign. When God is telling you not to advance, you feel a "check" or a sense of reluctance to proceed—that is your red light. If it feels right, then it's a green light.

When you look at something it may appear wonderful, even seem perfect—but when you pray about it, you might feel a resistance. That is the Holy Spirit telling you, "Don't do it." If we ignore the road signs and run the red light, we will hit something we won't like.

On the other hand, you may look at something, maybe a new job, and think that it doesn't look very good. You may have negative thoughts about the job—but when you pray about it, you may get a positive feeling. That is a green light from the Holy Spirit. God sees something in that job that you can't see and He knows that the end result will be for your good.

I've discovered that the greatest mistakes of my life happen when I stop listening to two people—the Holy Spirit and my wife. (Right, Dear?)

When we listen to the Holy Spirit, He will keep us from getting into the wrong stuff that brings heartache and problems. He will always lead us into things that are right and good for us.

YES! HE'S OUT OF THE BOX

God no longer lives in a golden box with angels on top of it, the Ark of the Covenant; rather, He lives by the Holy Spirit, in the human spirit regenerated by Christ. When you were saved, the Holy Spirit moved in; and when you became Spirit filled, the Holy Spirit brought with Him all the right furnishings.

The Holy Spirit was placed within you to make your life on earth not a perfect thing but a fruitful and beautiful thing.

The following Scripture reveals how the Bible expresses your ability to hear from God as the result of your relationship with Him:

> *Look! I stand at the door and knock.* **If you hear my voice and open the door**, *I will come in, and we will* **share a meal together as friends** (Revelation 3:20 NLT).

God is a gentleman; He is not shouting at you or banging on your door demanding entry. So the question is, will you answer the door? You have probably already opened the door of your heart to salvation. But...will you also open the door of your mind and spirit to hear what your Friend would say to you?

Every Christian, I believe, has heard God's voice—but few recognized it.

There are about 7 billion people on the earth and we each have our own personal way of expressing ourselves in our various languages. The Holy Spirit will talk to you in your particular lingo. Don't expect to hear, "Thus saith the Lord." No. He uses *your words* and things that are meaningful to communicate so that you can understand the subtle nuance of His meaning.

My wife likes hummingbirds and God speaks to her through her love for hummingbirds. I love sunsets; if you didn't know that, check out the many pictures of sunsets on my Facebook page. As a sunset fanatic, God speaks to me through sunsets. God knows my language and He knows yours, too. He knows how to speak to us using terms and images that we can relate to.

When you hear God's voice in your head, it will be the same voice used by your thoughts or inner dialogue. The skill we must acquire is the ability to discern His voice from our own.

It is the devil who wants you to believe that you cannot hear God's voice because you are not good enough, spiritual enough, or not enough in some other way.

Would you say aloud, right now, "I *can* hear God's voice. I *can* hear Him when He speaks to me." Repeat this phrase throughout your day until it becomes part of your belief system and inner dialogue. Don't listen to the liar and believe the devil's arguments. Every time you pray say, "Thank You, Father, that I *can* hear Your voice. Thank You, Holy Spirit, I *can* hear You when You speak to me."

YOUR HEAVENLY INTERMEDIARY

Now that Christ has returned to Heaven, the Holy Spirit is God's administrator of His interests, His Kingdom, and His will on the earth. It is the Holy Spirit's job to give the character of Christ and the power of Christ through the gifts of the Spirit to God's sons and daughters, you and me. Every day I pray and ask for all the gifts of the Spirit to operate in my life. I don't use all of them every day but I want them available.

The Bible tells us there are a total of eighteen spiritual gifts—and the Holy Spirit can't wait to share them with you. After all, it's His main job.

CHARISMATIC OR CRAZY-MATIC?

Charisma comes from the Greek word used in the Bible to mean "spiritual gifts." The word's meaning includes the thought of "grace," undeserved favor. As obvious as it may seem, we need to remember that "gifts" are not earned.

One of the primary references for spiritual gifts is found in First Corinthians, chapter 12. The very first verse presents a challenge to many wonderful Christian people: "*Now concerning spiritual gifts, brethren, I do not want you to be ignorant.*" Now connect that to Hosea 4:6: "*My people are destroyed for lack of knowledge….*"

The lack of knowledge concerning spiritual gifts, their importance, and place in the Church is the primary reason for writing this book. Many Christians understand salvation but are completely ignorant concerning spiritual gifts. Yet, according to Scripture, it is the empowering of believers through those gifts that will build God's Kingdom upon the earth.

The risen Christ, just before ascending to Heaven, gave explicit orders to His "believers." Since we are believers too, we have to consider these commands were also intended for us. Jesus said:

> *Go into all the world and **preach the gospel** to every creature. ...And these signs will follow those who believe: In My name they will **cast out demons**; they will **speak with new tongues**; they will take up serpents; and if they drink anything deadly, it will by no means hurt them; they will **lay hands on the sick**, and they will recover* (Mark 16:15-18).

So, we know from this Scripture that spreading the Good News isn't all we are to do, more is expected. The words *"will follow,"* speaking of the signs, mean we are expected to operate in the supernatural. In this Scripture Jesus mentions some of those *"signs"* and later in the New Testament the signs are called the gifts of the Spirit and they are explained in full.

YOUR PARTY FAVORS

Earlier we talked about parties only for the in-crowd and that nowadays God's party is for everyone. So let's talk about our party favors: *"But the manifestation of the Spirit is given to each one for the profit of all"* (1 Corinthians 12:7). Yes, God expects all of us to operate in the *"manifestation of the Spirit."*

Everyone can move in the gifts of the Spirit because all Christians can hear God's voice. Just because you don't think you've ever heard it does not mean that you haven't or that you can't.

There are nine gifts of the Spirit spoken of in First Corinthians 12:8-10:

> *For to one is given the **word of wisdom** through the Spirit, to another the **word of knowledge** through the same Spirit, to another **faith** by the same Spirit, to another **gifts of healings** by the same Spirit, to another the **working of miracles**, to another **prophecy**, to another **discerning of spirits**, to another **different kinds of tongues**, to another the **interpretation of tongues**.*

Each of us has spiritual gifts that we are more inclined toward. As I write this, I'm praying that the Holy Spirit will make known to you the gifts that you are predisposed toward. One of the gifts I'm inclined toward is prophecy.

One Sunday, while taking a power nap in the afternoon, I received a phone call. My wife answered it and woke me up to say that a world-famous minister wanted to speak to me. After ministering for five straight hours on Sunday morning, I often go home and take a power nap. Being deeply asleep when the man called, I wasn't at my sharpest when I answered the phone, but I didn't need to be.

When I took the phone, the man told me that he had another well-known person on the phone with us. He then asked me to prophesy over him. With eyes barely open and a mind still half asleep, I prophesied over him for fifteen minutes. Obviously, I don't have to work at operating in the gift of prophecy because it is one of the gifts I'm inclined toward.

You have an inclination for certain spiritual gifts, too. As you read on you can discover which ones.

THREE SPIRITUAL GIFT CATEGORIES

There are three categories of gifts revealed in First Corinthians, chapter 12: *Power Gifts, Revelation Gifts,* and *Utterance Gifts.* Within the power gifts, there are three subcategories: healings, working of miracles, faith. Within the revelation gifts there are also three subcategories: word of wisdom, word of knowledge, and discernment of spirits. Let's examine each of these in more detail.

POWER GIFTS—HEALINGS, WORKING OF MIRACLES, FAITH

HEALINGS

One of the power gifts is the gift of healings. I want you to notice that the word *healings* is plural. Healing is the supernatural restoration of some aspect of the human body to good health.

During several decades of experience with healing, I've learned that many people with this gift are most effective when bringing healing to a specific kind of health problem. I encourage you to ask God to show you what kind of illness you have the gift to heal and then go for it! Imagine what could happen if all the members of a church knew their specific healing gift and we could send those needing healing to the people with the appropriate healing anointing.

Working of Miracles

The Greek words for "working of miracles" are *energemata dunameon*. These are two very forceful words that mean energy and power. You may be familiar with the word *dunamis*, a derivative of *dunameon*, which is often used in the Bible when speaking of the miracle-working power of God.

The working of miracles is a temporary suspension of natural law by the Spirit of God to accomplish God's will in something that cannot be changed in the natural. The working of miracles is not just for healing. The times when Jesus walked on the water and fed the 5,000 are examples of the working of miracles.

Several years ago my church had an outreach to impoverished families in the community. We wanted every child to have a gift for Christmas, so we offered to provide disadvantaged children with gifts. The people brought their children who had signed up ahead of time, so we knew that 250 children would be attending. So, we purchased 250 gifts. We separated the gifts into two groups at the altar of the church, one stack of gifts for boys and one for girls.

When we opened the door for the event that day, people began streaming into the auditorium. They kept coming and coming! I stopped counting at about 700, and later we determined there were more than 800 children.

In a panic I rushed to my office looking for possible gifts. After deciding that the stapler on my desk wouldn't work, I considered going to Walmart, but there just wasn't enough time. So, I went back into the auditorium and in desperation prayed, "Lord, can You please help us out here?"

The children began going forward to get their gifts and about halfway through that process, I noticed something very peculiar. Even though about half the children had received their gifts, the gift piles remained the same! I mentioned this to a staff person and soon we were all standing around in shock watching the piles of gifts.

No thunder or lightning or spectacular event took place; the gifts simply never decreased! It wasn't what happened; it was what didn't happen. We gave gifts to more than 800 children and at the close of the night we still had 250 gifts remaining, the same amount we had at the beginning of the evening. Can you believe it? While I was having a nervous breakdown, obviously someone on the staff had the faith for this working of miracles.

Faith

Another power gift listed in First Corinthians 12 is the gift of faith. This is different from the faith you have as a believer, your common faith, your saving faith, your functioning faith. It is a special allocation of faith God gives for a brief period of time that is usually connected to the working of miracles. God gives people the gift of faith to take a bold action that in the natural is completely impossible. Most spectacular healings and miracles are preceded by someone having the gift of faith. This gift often works in partnership with other gifts.

The gift of faith is a supernaturally given capacity to believe God without any doubt for something that is impossible in the natural.

One time, years ago, while ministering in Germany with Lester Sumrall, we had more than 1,000 people answer an altar call for healing. Lester turned to me and said, "Go pray for them." I thought, *How in the world can I pray for a thousand people?* The assignment looked impossible; but the moment I stepped off the stage, the gift of faith filled me. The next thing I knew all the people at the altar fell to the floor as if they had been mowed down by a machine gun.

The power of God had pushed them to the floor. As I walked through the people, touching and praying for many of them, I came across a baby in the mother's arms. I took the baby from her and I prayed for the child although I didn't know what to pray for. Then I moved on to pray for others. I hadn't gone far when the lady with the baby began screaming at the top of her lungs. I thought to myself, *Did I drop the baby? What happened?*

Later, I watched as Dr Sumrall held up that same baby for all to see and said, "This baby came to the meeting without a right eyeball and had a deformed eye socket, and now look at her, she is perfect!" When I was praying for that baby I had supernatural faith.

REVELATION GIFTS—WORD OF WISDOM, WORD OF KNOWLEDGE, DISCERNMENT OF SPIRITS

The second type of spiritual gift mentioned in First Corinthians 12:8-10 is called the Revelation Gifts. They are the word of wisdom, word of knowledge, and discernment of spirits. Let's look at each one closely.

Word of Wisdom

A word of wisdom is given when God imparts supernatural insight to someone to accomplish His will in a specific thing. This gift often makes it possible for a person to do God's will by making the right decisions.

Most of the time, the word of wisdom has to do with the future. It is a present-future gift as opposed to the word of knowledge that is a present-past gift.

One day I was praying at home for a prosperous man in my church going through financial difficulties. I felt like I should call to check on him and when I did, he told me that things were looking up. The bank told him that he would not be losing his home. He had a very nice home in an exclusive area of Scottsdale, Arizona.

As soon as I got off the phone, the Lord spoke to me and said, "The bankers lied to him and Monday morning at 9 A.M. they will knock on his door and repossess his house to steal his equity." His house was worth three times his debt, millions of dollars.

The Lord told me to tell the man to contact his attorney to do what was necessary to protect his property. I called him back with that word of wisdom. He contacted his lawyer as the Lord suggested and got everything ready for Monday.

Monday morning around nine o'clock there was a knock on his door. He opened it to find six bankers who said they were there to repossess his home. He smiled and handed them the papers his lawyer had prepared. The greedy bankers stood there in shock as he closed the door in their faces and on their attempt to steal from him. A word of wisdom saved his home. The Holy Spirit will help you in all of life's decisions when you ask for a word of wisdom.

Word of Knowledge

God is omniscient, all knowing. With the word of knowledge, we can discern things that we could never be aware of without God's help. Personally, I love this gift because it has been active in my life and God has shown me how to use it to bring help and healing to those in need.

The gift of the word of knowledge is a small fragment of God's "database" of information that we can access to bring healing, deliverance, guidance, protection, and provision into people's lives.

One day while praying, I asked God to show me His might. I immediately had a vision of a massive, rapidly moving river. It was so large that I couldn't see all the way across it. The river was beautiful and when the waters slowed down, I could tell that it wasn't a river of water as I had supposed, but a river of thoughts. It was the mind of God. Then God spoke to me and said, "You can't contain all that is within My mind, but when you need a word of knowledge, just reach in and gather a handful of information. It will be more than enough for your needs."

One of the first times I used a word of knowledge was when I was a young associate pastor at my father's church in California. We had a wonderful woman in the church whose playboy son only attended church with her on Mother's Day. He was a six-foot-six, handsome guy who drove a Porsche and was a millionaire.

He had an attitude against God but he loved his mom. One Mother's Day morning, I had a vision of him as a 12-year-old boy standing over his father's casket. The Lord told me that he had never gotten over his father's death and that he blamed God for killing his father. God told me, "Tell him today that I didn't do that and I love him and I don't want him angry at Me anymore."

At the end of the service, I revealed to him my vision of him standing over his father's casket. I said, "I saw your heart break and you get angry at God. God told me to tell you that He didn't kill your father and He misses having a relationship with you." Immediately, the playboy millionaire fell to his knees and gave his heart to the Lord. One little sliver of knowledge changed everything.

The devil can't do that, false religion can't do that— only God can reach people through this gift when nothing else can. The Holy Spirit has a key to unlock the hearts of people if you will just allow Him to use you.

Discernment of Spirits

Another revelation gift is discernment of spirits, which is supernatural insight into the true nature of the people or spirits operating in a given situation whether they be angels, demons, or God. When you know which spirit is operating, you can be protected and wise in your dealing with a person or situation.

I was 21, and Mary and I had been married only a short time when we visited a new church. We were seated in the back row when the Holy Spirit started talking to me concerning the pastor. He said, "That man has an unclean spirit. He is attracted to other men and I don't want you to open your spirit to his ministry." I told Mary that I felt we should leave immediately because there is something wrong with the minister, so we left.

By nature, I'm a gullible and naïve person. I'm not on the lookout for people with an agenda. I know that comes naturally to some, but for me it's just too much work. I've found that through the gift of discernment of spirits, God will protect even those of us who are naïve. He will keep us safe from controlling and manipulating people and those who operate in witchcraft.

UTTERANCE GIFTS

There are also spiritual gifts called utterance gifts—tongues, interpretation of tongues, and prophecy. I'll speak more about these in later chapters, but I want to briefly introduce them.

The utterance gifts are divinely inspired communications that bring encouragement and healing to others. It is a manifestation of the Holy Spirit and not of human intellect.

When I was an assistant pastor at a church in Gilbert, Arizona, the wife of a very successful farmer was a regular attendee. Occasionally, her husband came with her although he wasn't a Christian. He was a mountain of a man who wore overalls to church. Although he seemed very nice, he was so physically large that he was intimidating.

Prior to a service one day, I was in my office at the church praying in tongues when the gift of tongues began to operate in me. The tongues came out so forcefully that I was shouting and had to grab a pillow from the couch to cover my mouth. It only lasted two or three minutes.

Perhaps I should explain that the gift of tongues is not the same as your prayer language.

Soon afterward, I went into the service and I was preaching when the Holy Spirit interrupted me. I walked off the stage because I felt like I should, but really had no idea what I was doing. I walked up to this six-foot-eight, 350-pound farmer in his overalls and gave him a word from God.

He began to violently weep and the entire church also began to weep as he gave his heart to Christ. Then the Lord said to me, "This man's salvation began before the service while you were praying." I realized that God was talking about the gift of tongues that had come on me before church. My words to the man were the interpretation of those tongues. Truly, amazing things can happen when we allow the Holy Spirit to function in us.

I spent some wonderful time with Oral Roberts before his death, and on one occasion he told me a great story: A friend of his had some land in Tulsa that he wanted Oral Roberts to look at. While viewing it, he began speaking in tongues. A moment later when he interpreted the message God said, "Build me a great university here so that I can send students to the nations to bring healing." It was due to the gift of tongues and interpretation that he knew God wanted him to build Oral Roberts University. The gifts of tongues and interpretation of tongues have the same outcome as prophecy.

All believers should seek to be used in the gift of prophecy. It is an activation point for every believer and the entry point gift to the other spiritual gifts.

One of the reasons why God wants the Church to become prophetic is because He wants all the other gifts to become active, too. Once you learn to allow the Holy Spirit to function through you in prophecy, it becomes easier to operate in the other gifts. I will go into greater detail about the gift of prophecy in upcoming chapters.

AWARENESS AND ACTIVATION

I have found that praying in the Spirit is a key to activating the spiritual gifts in your life.

> But one and the same Spirit works all these things, **distributing** [gifts] **to each one individually** *as He wills* (1 Corinthians 12:11).

Please notice the phrase *"to each one"* in this verse. If you are born again, that verse of Scripture includes you. Resident within you is an inclination toward at least two and possibly three gifts of the Spirit and one of them is your dominant gift.

Earlier in this chapter I mentioned that I was praying that you would discover the spiritual gifts that God has given you. Now that you understand more about spiritual gifts, I want you to ask yourself if God has stirred your heart concerning any of these gifts. Have you felt an affinity or an appetite for any of them to operate in your life?

Would you pray aloud with me concerning your spiritual gifts:

> *Holy Spirit, thank You for helping me find my dominant or primary gift. The one I am most predisposed to. I lay claim to that spiritual gift and all others that You intend for me. I want to function in it. I desire to flow in it, and I hunger to be used of You through it because I long to make a difference. More than anything I want to hear Your voice and follow where You lead me in operating in my gifts. Amen.*

Chapter 3

Dos and Don'ts for Prophetic Folk

Ezekiel 37 verses 1 through 14 tell of a vision God gave to the prophet Ezekiel. God placed him in a valley filled with stacks of dry bones and then asked him an odd question: *"Son of man, can these bones live?"* Ezekiel replied cautiously, *"O Lord God, You know."*

Then God commanded Ezekiel, *"Prophesy to these bones, and say to them, 'O dry bones, hear the word of the Lord!'"* You probably know the rest of the story, the prophet did as God commanded and amazingly the bones came together to form human bodies; but the re-created people still lay on the ground dead.

Then God commanded Ezekiel to call to the four winds to come and restore the breath of life to the dead beings. The Bible says, "...*breath came into them, and they lived, and stood upon their feet, an exceedingly great army.*"

God's will has to be spoken. When God wants to do something on the earth, He will give an earth person the authority and power to speak out His will. That is precisely the reason that God made it possible for born-again people to prophesy. He wants to use us to declare His will on the earth.

I know people who have traveled around the world to places they felt God wanted them to go to prophesy the things He told them to say. They would speak out the will of God concerning a particular location. We need to understand that when we speak something God has said to us, it becomes dynamic. By launching those "words" into the appropriate environment, we make it possible for God to do what He said prophetically He would do.

It may take a day, a month, or a century later when someone walks under the umbrella of that prophetic promise and begins to accomplish the thing that someone else released prophetically. God's power resides in that place waiting for the right person at the right time to come along to accomplish His purposes.

CALL FORTH THE KINGDOM

God said to Ezekiel, let's get everything needed to create an army and told him to prophesy to the bones to come together. Ezekiel did what the Lord commanded and the scattered bones came together. Then Ezekiel was told to prophesy for muscle and sinew to cover the bones and it happened. I'm sure that included tissue and organs and everything necessary to make a complete person. Then God told him to prophesy breath into their lungs, and they came alive.

This vision illustrates that for God's will to be accomplished there are often various levels, dimensions, and degrees that must be completed. For example, in your own life God will talk to you about the next thing to come. Once that happens, He'll talk to you about the following thing—but very rarely will God lay out your entire life for you in complete detail. Almost always there is a progression toward the end goal God wants to accomplish. That is how He usually moves and advances us and it is also how He manifests His will on the earth.

As God works incrementally in your life, you may not see how each thing moves you in the direction of His will—some things may even seem to be setbacks. But always remember that God makes *"…all things work together for good to those who love God, to those who are the called according to His purpose"* (Romans 8:28).

Through Ezekiel's vision we learned that God wants to speak the things He would do on the earth through His people before doing them. Also, we learned that God usually achieves His will on the earth incrementally.

PROPHECY, THE TWO-EDGED SWORD

Psalm 149:6 says, *"Let the high praises of God be in their mouth, and a two-edged sword in their hand."* This is the picture of what a soldier, a believer, in God's Kingdom looks like—a worshipper armed with a prophetic word that cuts two ways.

The phrase for two-edged sword in the Greek literally means "two-mouthed sword." A prophecy is like a two-edged sword in that it first cuts into us when we hear the word and releases something new in us. That, however, is only half the value of that prophetic word. Anything God gives you isn't just to speak to you, it is meant to cut another way and be a second mouth when it speaks to others.

Prophecy elevates you to a platform of spiritual influence only limited by God. So, as a son or daughter of God, you have the authority to speak prophetically into any situation and even to the nations.

I've learned to use the prophecies God has given me in my personal prayer life. I love to remind the devil of the things God has said. I just speak what God told me prophetically. I say, "Devil, you're in serious trouble because

God told me...." These are things God has spoken to me about my life, my family members, and the church. When I speak those words from God, it is like a sword shoots out of my mouth to overcome anything that would hinder their fulfillment...and you can do the same.

ALPHABET IN = LOGOS OUT

The Word of God within us is the key to prophecy flowing out of us. (Please read that sentence again.) Obviously, to prophesy you have to hear from God. That means there is nothing more important to a believer than fueling your spirit with God's Word, the truths in the Bible. What God speaks to you through His Word and during times of prayer, He is ready to release through you. As God's word flows into you, the Holy Spirit will make it into sentences that flow out of you, if you will allow it.

Luke 6:45 (NLT) explains how this works:

> *A good person produces good things from the treasury of a good heart, and an evil person produces evil things from the treasury of an evil heart. What you say flows from what is in your heart.*

Since what we hear is important to prophesying, we must ask ourselves, "What and who are we listening to?" Are we spending time reading God's Word and in prayer listening for His voice, or do we primarily fill our minds with our work, relationships, entertainment, the Internet, the news, etc.? None of those things are bad, they just cannot be the primary focus of our attention if we want to prophesy.

People who move in prophecy, yet are deficient in the Word of God are vulnerable to a host of errors. When they reach out for a prophetic word, they can end up saying things that aren't scriptural and not even know the difference.

Here is an important principle to remember: a prophetic word will never contradict God's written Word, the Bible. If it does, it is not a legitimate prophecy from God. Any doctrine, belief, or practice that is not revealed in Scripture cannot be established through a prophecy.

GOTTA HAVE FAITH

Romans 12:6 says, *"Having then gifts differing according to the grace that is given to us, let us use them: if prophecy, let us prophesy in proportion to our faith."* Okay, we need to have our faith built up in order to prophesy, and Scripture gives us the formula for increasing our faith: *"So then faith comes by hearing, and hearing by the word of God"* (Romans 10:17).

The level of your faith is equal to the level of God's Word within you. In prophecy, you can't go above where you are in the Word. Prophecy comes out after the Word of God goes in.

Want to prophesy? Then you have to become a serious and consistent reader and studier of the Bible. However, we prophesy not according to the amount of Word we have read, but in proportion to the amount of Word in which we live.

DIFFERENT STROKES FOR DIFFERENT PROPHETIC FOLKS

I believe God wants every Christian to become prophetic, but I realize that they will express their gift in different ways. Very few people will have the opportunity to stand on a church platform during a service and speak. However, God provides prophetic outlets and has prophetic styles that are appropriate for everyone and their circumstances.

An ideal prophetic opportunity for many can be found in small groups. If you are not a member of a small Bible study or cell group in your church, you might be missing an important opportunity to prophesy. And what about when someone takes a seat next to you in church, is it possible that God could have put the person there because He has something prophetic for you to say? What about the person standing next to you in the checkout line?

Sometimes a Scripture comes to mind that a believer feels impressed to share with a particular person. Others will have thoughts or insights they know are from God for someone. Others will have prophetically inspired prayers that need to be declared over a person, place, or thing. Prophecy has many expressions, and no one has to copy anyone else.

LEAP INTO THE RIVER OF REVELATION

In another vision, found in Ezekiel 47:1-12, God showed Ezekiel a stream of water coming out from under the temple flowing toward the sea. When Ezekiel checked it out, he discovered the water got deeper the farther out he went. At first it was ankle deep, and then knee deep, then waist deep, and soon it was over his head. This vision depicts how the Holy Spirit moves in the lives of Christian people.

Some Christians and denominations are merely ankle deep in the waters of the Holy Spirit. They are in the beginning stages of the river. They have found salvation and they are splashing around and calling it glorious. It *is* glorious that we are born again, but there is so much more and yet many don't realize it. Their full spiritual potential is never known or of benefit to the Kingdom because they are satisfied to be ankle deep in the beginning stage of God's river of revelation.

We have to realize that what we call revival and have seen in the past isn't even swimming waters for the "last days" revival. There is a lot more the Holy Spirit wants to do than we have heard of, seen, or experienced in the past. So we have to dare to go beyond the safety of the waters we know and dive in deeper to find the revival that the Holy Spirit wants to bring to our day.

As Ezekiel moved deeper into the waters, he noticed that the river was pulling on him and he had to fight more and more to remain in control. The greater the river of the Holy Spirit tries to influence us, the more we struggle to remain on top of things.

PROPHETIC MISTAKES

Some people fear that if we open up the church to prophecy that when new people prophesy they will make mistakes…and that may happen. However, prophecy is like everything else, you only become good at something by practicing, and that means making a few mistakes. However, mistakes that occur where there is pastoral oversight can be corrected and no harm done. Yes, you may get it wrong sometimes, but at least you tried.

On one occasion, I was prophesying to two women who knew each other and were standing next to one another. After speaking to the first lady, I turned to prophesy to the other one. When I finished, they looked at each other then looked at me kind of funny and told me that I had their prophecies turned around. The word I gave to the first lady was actually for the second lady and vice versa.

HOW DEEP ARE YOU?

When the water is up to your waist, you are halfway in— but you are also halfway out. You may be at this point. It is a difficult stage because you know that God wants all of you, but you are allowing "things" like fear for example, to hold you back. If that is where *you* are concerning prophecy, there can be only one answer—ask God to forgive you and plunge into the deep and expect Him to help you with every difficulty that arises.

"Waters to swim in" is the next stage and where God wants you to be. This is when you completely give in to the current of the Holy Spirit and allow prophecy and other spiritual gifts to flow in your life. We need to learn to allow the currents of the Spirit to take us and move us wherever God desires.

There are stages and levels of God's Spirit. In these last days, God is giving a deeper and fuller measure of the experience of His presence and power than at any time before. He wants to show the world His glory through us. This means that not just preachers are going to raise the dead and do wildly supernatural things—ordinary Christians will get to do the cool stuff too! You don't need special permission to move in the supernatural, you already have an engraved invitation in God's Word.

TEST BEFORE TASTING

First Thessalonians 5:21 says, *"Test all things; hold fast what is good."* I was eating salmon the other day and found a small bone in it so I picked up my plate, dashed it against the wall and shouted, "I will never eat salmon again!" Just kidding, I did *not* do that. Instead, I picked out the tiny bone, put it aside, and enjoyed the rest of the meat.

We are to do the same thing with a prophecy. The gift of prophecy, like every spiritual gift, has a growth phase. Those who are new to prophecy can mix their own personality, history, feelings, and personal beliefs into a prophetic word.

Most prophecies given by inexperienced people almost always have something from God, but they may also have something from themselves mixed in it.

Some people say that if any part of a prophecy is wrong then none of it can be true; or if a prophet gets something wrong, the person can never again be trusted to say what is right. Those two views are very wrong.

That would be like me saying to a daughter that I am teaching to drive and who just ran over a curb, "Yea, thus sayeth your father, though you drove several blocks well, you just hit a curb so you are permanently disqualified from driving forever and ever and ever. Amen." No. Just like learning to drive, we learn from our mistakes and get back behind the wheel and do it again—and the more we do it, the better we get at it.

At our church we don't believe in "parking lot prophecy" because it lacks accountability. We don't want anything done in the shadows. If someone tells you they have a word for you and says, "But don't tell the pastor." My word for you is, "By all means tell the pastor." Test everything you hear, even what you hear from the pulpit; check it against the Bible.

If you believe that you have a prophetic word for someone, take another person with you who is spiritually discerning enough to check the credibility of your word when you give it.

How to Verify a Prophetic Word

First, if a prophecy is from God it will bear witness with you. Prophetic words are almost always a confirmation of something you have already heard from God; and when you hear it, there will be a "leaping" inside you.

Remember when Mary the mother-to-be of Jesus went to visit her cousin Elizabeth who was pregnant with John the Baptist? The Bible says that Elizabeth's baby leaped in her womb (Luke 1:41). This is an example of the witness of the Holy Spirit within you that you often experience when someone gives you a true prophetic word.

Second, ask yourself if the prophecy lines up with Scripture. God will never tell you to do something in a prophecy that the Bible says is wrong. For example, God will never tell you to leave your spouse to marry someone else. That may sound obvious to you, but we can all be tempted to accept a word that is against Scripture if it gives us the way out of a difficult situation or meets some deep need.

Third, submit any word given to you to your pastoral spiritual coverage for evaluation. If your pastor is a real man of God, he will be able to accurately judge the word given you.

Fourth, ask yourself if the person giving the word is morally clean. The Bible does not tell us to judge others by their gift but by their fruit. What kind of fruit is their lifestyle producing? There is a tendency in charismatic circles to elevate people because of their gift and be blind to their moral failures.

PITFALLS FOR PROPHETS

First Thessalonians 5:19-20 explains how to move in the realm of the gifts of the Spirit by telling us what *not* to do. It says, *"Do not quench the Spirit. Do not despise prophecies."* We *quench* the Spirit by stopping the fullness of the Spirit's gifts from operating in us and in our churches. We *grieve* the Spirit by our character flaws or sin. These things distance us from God.

I believe the day is coming when more and more churches will welcome the Holy Spirit by making place for His gifts during their services.

We must be obedient, humble, and teachable to develop our spiritual gifts. A major pitfall for those learning to use their gifts is pride. When God does something supernatural through us, we can easily be amazed by our spiritual gift and forget that we are merely God's mouthpiece.

Prophecy can cause some people to feel special and important. The fact is that you *are* special and important, but not because you prophesy. Being a worshipper will help you to reverse pride and keep it in check. Those who operate in spiritual gifts and are not worshippers can become prideful. Worship, however, reminds us what is what and who is who; it keeps us balanced.

Finally—when God gives us a word for someone, we should not use it to make ourselves look good. Rather, we should ask the Lord to show us how to tie the prophecy into meeting the person's needs. We should always strive to use our gift as a tool to build up others and God's Kingdom...not ourselves.

Chapter 4

MUSIC EMPOWERS
THE PROPHETIC

Music was created by God and is an important part
of the makeup of Heaven. In fact, the very presence
of God is infused with music. Congregations of
angels continually create music that declares God's
goodness and the glory of His majestic presence.
Spiritually enriched music is a key to hearing the
prophetic and to infusing prophetic proclamations
with a world-changing power.

MUSIC IS INFECTIOUS

Music is a powerful container, transmitter, and opener. Whether you can "carry a tune" or not, music has a great effect on a person's life. Music, both instrumental and vocal, transmits what is in the spirit of the artist to the audience. This spiritual transmission is something that most people do not grasp and is often misunderstood. What is in the spirit of a musician is broadcast into the listener through music. Therefore, Christians must be cautious about what they listen to and thereby assimilate into their lives.

I'm not being nitpicky or religious about your favorite secular music. I merely want to warn you that through music you can unknowingly receive problems into your life. For example, if you listen to the music of a person with an immoral lifestyle, you may find yourself struggling or tempted by those same issues due to the spiritual transference from their music.

Music can cause you to accept an idea that you would normally reject. When you hear something spoken, you judge and logically analyze it. However, if you hear those same words in music, the thoughts those words contain are not analyzed. They bypass the intellect and acceptance can occur.

Spiritual music, because it is spiritual, is powerful. God created music to have a spiritual force. Consequently, it can be a great influence for good or for evil.

THE EVIL MUSIC MASTER

It is worth noting that the greatest musician ever created was named lucifer. He is the fallen angel we refer to as the devil. He was the choir leader over one third of the heavenly host whose job was to worship God. The Bible says that he was like a beautiful organ.

Lucifer was so musical that he couldn't speak without creating music. Everything he said he sang, and his voice contained a great orchestra of sounds. In addition, he was translucent and the beautiful gems God placed inside him created a light show. So, as well as worshipping God musically, lucifer also worshipped visually. Whenever lucifer came into God's presence leading the millions of worshipping angels, not only did his organ pipes produce beautiful sounds of worship but he also generated beautiful rays of light in a rainbow of colors.

When this worship leader fell to earth, he never lost sight of the influence music has on the soul. Satan has tried to use music as a tool for the destruction of humankind rather than as a tool for good. Almost every activity satan is involved in has an accompanying musical sound.

Please don't think that I'm referring to "heavy metal" music. I'm not talking about a song's musical style but about its spirit. Many of the fallen angels we call demons also have musical abilities. Almost all people who kill themselves, commit violent acts, or behave in an obsessive manner has some kind of music that stimulates or accompanies their actions.

Satan uses his musical gift to deceive humankind in an attempt to destroy God's purpose for their lives.

THE PRAISE PROTOCOL

Music in its highest form is a pathway to God's presence.

David teaches us there is a protocol to entering God's presence—we are to enter with worship and leave with worship. David instructs: *"Shout with joy to the Lord, all the earth! Worship the Lord with gladness. Come before him, singing with joy"* (Psalm 100:1-2 NLT). David was declaring there is a progression to coming before God—we come into His presence with singing and we open the gate to His glorious presence with thanksgiving.

Thanksgiving is thanking God for our salvation, healing, deliverance, His Word, His love, the gift of His Spirit, and more. We enter His presence with a declaration of God's accomplishments, what He has done for us personally and what He has done for all humankind.

David says that we should go beyond "thanksgiving" into "praise," which is moving to a higher dimension in worship. Praise isn't thanking God for what He has done but honoring Him for His divine attributes. Praise addresses the person and not the works of God. We proclaim who He is. For example, "You, Lord, are wonderful, glorious, good, and Your mercies endure forever."

It is important to become knowledgeable and skilled in worshipping God for His attributes because much of the Church is ignorant of the magnitude of God's divine qualities. When you become aware of one of God's attributes and praise Him for it, the recognition of that attribute creates a desire within you for that same quality to manifest in your life.

Many Christians yearn to know how to "walk in the Spirit." The secret is being constantly filled with the Holy Spirit and to continually worship God. Paul admonishes us to:

> *...Be filled with the Spirit, speaking to one another in psalms and hymns and spiritual songs, singing and making melody in your heart to the Lord, giving thanks always for all things to God the Father in the name of our Lord Jesus Christ* (Ephesians 5:18-20).

PASSAGEWAY TO HIS PRESENCE

Music can create a direct connect to God. You may be thinking, *But, Pastor, I'm not very musical...so that won't work for me.* If you can whistle, clap your hands, hum in your heart, or even move your toes in time to the music, you are musical enough to connect with God. In fact, you don't even have to be able to carry a tune. God doesn't hear the quality of your voice—He is listening to the purity of the praise coming from your heart.

Music has the power to change the environment and atmosphere, for good or for bad. Wherever you go, you should carry with you a song in your heart not only to keep in touch with God but also to shield you from evil.

David shows us that praise can even drive out evil spirits:

> *But the Spirit of the Lord departed from Saul, and a distressing spirit from the Lord troubled him. ....And so it was, whenever the spirit from God was upon Saul, that David would take a harp and play it with his hand. Then Saul would become refreshed and well, and the distressing spirit would depart from him* (1 Samuel 16:14,23).

There is more to this story than a soothing song calming a troubled spirit. David's music was spiritual and had a supernatural effect on Saul.

When an anointed person plays a musical note, that note carries something spiritual to you whether they sing it or not. This is why you will feel a heightened expression of God's presence when you are in a worship service conducted by a person anointed to lead worship.

You may have been to churches where the worship leader was gifted and talented in the natural, but you didn't feel much spiritually during their worship. An anointed person can sing the same song as one without the unction or anointing, and the spiritual results will be as different as day and night. Yes, the words of a song are important, but it is the anointing that makes the difference.

POWER OF THE WORSHIP-SPHERE

When I was a young man, one night I was leading an all-night prayer and worship service for the young people in my dad's church. At about 2:30 in the morning we were startled by a loud knocking on the front door. The auditorium lights couldn't be seen from the street and we had parked in the back of the church. There wasn't any reason why anyone passing by would know we were there. Everyone stared at me, so I figured I was nominated to answer the door.

I opened the door to find a well-dressed man whose Cadillac was parked behind him. He looked at me with great intensity as tears streamed down his face. He told me his name and then said, "I'm a backslidden pastor. I've just come from a drug situation, but while driving past this church something compelled me to drive into the parking lot. I couldn't go an inch farther or a minute longer without coming here."

What had happened? During our worship we created a sphere that was filled with the presence of God and when the man drove through that environment, the demon spirit who ruled his life had to leave.

The man knelt down right there at the doorway of our church and repented and gave his life back to God. We prayed over him and continued our worship with a new awe for the power of the presence of God. Together we had created a spiritual environment, and when he came into it his life was changed.

This is why it is so important that you not be passive in a worship environment. Your praise is the key to someone's deliverance. Your worship affects not only you but other people. The more people involved in worship, the wider and more powerful that life-changing spiritual ambiance becomes. Worship is one way we can bring forth God's power and lordship over a city.

WORSHIP IS YOUR COMBAT ASSIGNMENT

In Second Chronicles there is a time when the nation of Israel was surrounded by three armies. Israel's army was outnumbered 10 to 1. In the natural it looked hopeless. In desperation, King Jehoshaphat prayed to God for deliverance. God responded through a prophet saying:

...Do not be afraid nor dismayed because of this great multitude, for the battle is not yours, but God's. You will not need to fight in this battle. ...Do not fear or be dismayed; tomorrow go out against them, for the Lord is with you (2 Chronicles 20:15,17).

Then the king and all the people bowed to the ground and worshipped God and the Bible says that afterward, they "*...stood to praise the Lord, the God of Israel, with a very loud shout*" (2 Chronicles 20:19 NLT). They received a word and they worshipped, and the next day they went out to battle as God had commanded. Israel's army was led by a band of worshippers singing, *"Praise the Lord, for His mercy endures forever"* (2 Chronicles 20:21).

They sang this song of worship over and over again while playing their instruments. As they worshipped, the Bible says that God *"set ambushes"* against the opposing armies and they began fighting one another. By the time the army of Israel arrived at the battlefield, all they saw was a battleground filled with the dead bodies of their foes. The Bible says that not a single enemy soldier escaped. Their worship had invited angels to intervene in a way that caused their enemies to destroy themselves (2 Chronicles 20:22-24).

We can learn from this story a formula to use when we come upon difficult times. First, they prayed. Second, they heard from God. Third, they worshipped. Then God changed everything.

YOUR "NEW SONG"

One of the words for *praise* in the Hebrew language is *tehila,* which literally means "spontaneous songs of adoration." You may remember that when David was king he brought the Ark of the Covenant to Jerusalem, placed it in a tent, and caused there to be continuous worship. While the musicians were singing praises, they received new songs and a priest was stationed there to write them down. This method of obtaining new ideas and fresh insights can work in every area of our lives. While in God's presence during worship, God can give you new ideas and renew your strength, your life, your joy, your peace, and your love.

A church that is really experiencing God presence can't help itself from expressing new and creative worship music.

David says in Psalm 98:1: *"Sing to the Lord a new song! For He has done marvelous things; His right hand and His holy arm have gained Him the victory."*

The admonition to sing a *"new song"* is found over and over again throughout Scripture. I love the old songs; there is nothing wrong with them or with singing them. However, God encourages us to make our praise current, new, and fresh. God always wants to do something new in us, for us, and through us—and out of our willingness to receive a new song, marvelous new things will spontaneously come…if we allow them.

When a move of God begins to die, its music loses it newness and becomes about the glory experienced in the past.

New songs can be in any style, rock, rap, classical, jazz, country, and other types. God doesn't have just one sound. If you listen to a new song with your spirit, ignoring your song-style preference and even the mistakes of an unskilled musician, you can hear inspiring praise and worship to God.

It is natural to love old worship songs that are meaningful to you, but don't ignore the new stuff. New songs represent what God is doing today. To turn your back on them is to risk becoming spiritually stagnate and miss what God is doing now.

THE POWER OF PROPHETIC MUSIC

*Moreover David and the captains of the army separated for the service some of the sons of Asaph, of Heman, and of Jeduthun, who should **prophesy with harps, stringed instruments, and cymbals**… (1 Chronicles 25:1).*

As said at the beginning of this chapter, music is a medium that carries things within it. When an anointed person worships on an instrument, the notes themselves carry a message. Even without words, the sounds of worship can invoke the presence of God. So when an anointed musical note comes to the hearers and they receive it, supernatural things can happen. They can experience healing, joy, peace, and more.

In Second Kings 3 we find the prophet Elisha confronted by two kings who wanted a word from God. The king of Israel and the king of Judah were planning to make war together on the neighboring country of Moab, and they wanted God's wisdom about the success of their enterprise. (This was during the time when Israel was divided.) They ask Elisha for a prophetic word. Because one king was a godly man and the other was not, Elisha had a hard time hearing from God. He needed help.

So, Elisha asked that a harp player be brought to play for him. He was asking for an anointed musician. The Bible says: "*...Then it happened, when the musician played, that the hand of the Lord came upon him*" (2 Kings 3:15). The anointed music made it possible for Elisha to hear from God and tell them that Israel's war would be successful.

Once again we see that anointed worship opens the heavens. It opens access to hear a prophetic word and to know God's heart and mind. During times of worship, listen for God to speak to you, too.

David—Worshipper, Warrior, and Inventor?

David was not only a great worshipper; he was also a great warrior. However, he didn't claim to have learned to fight from some great soldier or through his own natural ability, he stated that God taught him to fight: *"He teaches my hands to make war, so that my arms can bend a bow of bronze"* (Psalm 18:34). David warred as much with worship as he did with a slingshot, sword, and bow.

In addition, we know that King David invented at least twenty-six instruments. As David worshipped, perhaps he thought, *God is speaking something within me that is beyond this instrument's ability to express,* and the concept for a new instrument of worship would be born. It was David's hunger for worship that released a creative explosion of inventions, primarily of stringed instruments.

Worship-Guided Missiles

When we persist in praise, an elevation of worship occurs. Worship changes from thanksgiving to praise, and from praise to adoration, and then it can inspire the prophetic within those who are listening for it. Because God is enmeshed in our worship, we move from the earthly realm of singing and making music into a heavenly realm where all things are possible.

The higher people ascend in praise and worship, the more authoritative their prophetic declarations are. At the height of heavenly worship we should declare prophetic words we have received from God. At that time they reach farther and are more powerful and effective.

We have yet to fully grasp this truth and to use it to experience the results that are possible. I believe that the "last days" Church will become more and more effective in using this weapon to expand God's Kingdom and bring His will to the earth. These believers will learn how to generate high praise and declare words from God that will change nations.

> *Let the high praises of God be in their mouth,*
> *and a two-edged sword in their hand* (Psalm
> 149:6).

The Church has to stop thinking it is impotent, powerless, without a voice, and that we have lost the ability to influence our nation.

The most powerful people in the world today are prophetic believers because they have access to God. What we have not fully understood is that everyone is prophetic and therefore everyone has the ability to release God's will to nations, to generations, and to the entire world.

Now is the time for us, the prophetic Christians, to discover the power we possess through prophetic worship. It is time to use our God-given power to fulfill our assignment to bring God's Kingdom to the earth.

Chapter **5**

PROPHECY—
THE MEANS TO
YOUR DESTINY

*This **charge** I **commit** to you, son Timothy, **according to the prophecies** previously made **concerning you**, that by them **you may wage the good warfare**, having faith and a good conscience, which some having rejected, concerning the faith have suffered shipwreck* (1 Timothy 1:18-19).

Paul begins the topic of this conversation with Timothy by using the word *charge*. The Greek word translated as *charge* means "mandate, a command." Then Paul's following statements are even stronger using the word *commit*. When Timothy read this letter, the words *charge* and *commit* must have leaped off the page at him. He knew that he was getting his marching order from his spiritual father.

Later in that sentence, Paul explains that the prophetic words Timothy received were filled with supernatural energy and backed by the very power of Heaven to accomplish their purpose. However, until Timothy fully received and utilized them, they were merely dusty weapons hidden under the bed. Paul is challenging Timothy to reclaim his prophetic inheritance.

By allowing this letter to be part of the Holy Bible, God is emphasizing to us, too, this vital spiritual truth. Like Paul did Timothy, God commits a charge to us to live by an important spiritual principle. God is saying, "I charge you to stop ignoring the prophecies given to you, stop diminishing them, and stop allowing them to be unused weapons in your spiritual arsenal. It is time for you to fully understand the power of prophecy and activate it by your faith."

Dust off the prophetic words you've been given and get them ready for warfare.

NO PROPHETIC WORDS?

Many have given the word *prophecy* a super-duper spiritual meaning that puts it in a class reserved for extremely gifted, talented, and "holy" people. Consider this question: What does the word *prophecy* mean? Doesn't it simply mean God speaking to a person?

You might be thinking, *Wow, all that sounds really good but none of this teaching actually pertains to me because I have never been given a prophecy.* I beg to differ.

A prophecy doesn't have to be a "Thus sayeth the Lord…" kind of word. It can also be something you heard during a message that spoke to your heart or something you read in your Bible that stood out to you.

God speaks to everyone, which of course includes you, who reads the Scriptures. When something you read comes alive to you, God has given you a prophecy. Also, when listening to a sermon, God will often emphasize something that is said. You may even get so engrossed in that thought that you miss the rest of the sermon. And, that is okay because God was speaking to you, and that too is prophecy.

HOW I ROLL

When I was founding my church in Scottsdale, Arizona, I rented a building without getting the city's approval to have a church there. Now you may think that was foolish, but I knew God was calling me to Scottsdale. I found what I felt was the place God had for us to meet, so I rented it. That's just how I roll.

However, the city of Scottsdale refused to "roll" with me. The property was located in an industrial area, and Scottsdale had never previously allowed a church to be established in an industrial or retail area. I requested approval five times and was turned down each time.

As I sat in an airport waiting for a flight, I was disappointed and wondering if I had missed something from God. Then a friend sat down beside me, tapped me on the shoulder, and told me that he had a word for me. His word wasn't what I expected—it was five Scriptures concerning supernatural favor.

I did not reapply for the zoning exception, but for the next ten days I beat the devil's brains out with that prophetic word, those five Scriptures. I said, "Listen devil, I'm walking in favor and you cannot keep me from my God-given destiny! Listen to this Scripture…. Now listen to this one…" and I didn't stop until I'd declared all five Scriptures to him.

On the eleventh day, I received a call from someone at the city zoning commission. The man said, "Pastor Maiden, we've decided, on our own initiative and without your request, to let you have a church in that industrial park…and by the way, we're going to pay for the permit. Have a nice day." And I did—praising and thanking God for His favor.

Declaring a prophetic word and having God's will come about didn't happen because I'm a pastor. It happened because I took what had been given to me prophetically and hammered the devil with it until it became reality.

You have the right to do the very same thing. It wasn't my job title that caused it to happen it was the power in the prophetic word I'd been given. Yes, *you* can "roll" the same way.

PROPHECY IS A SPIRITUAL ENDOWMENT

If you have had a prophecy spoken to you and knew that it was real or received a word from God in any other way, then understand this—that prophetic word was meant to be more than an encouragement for your mind or a comfort for troubled emotions. It certainly can be all that, but it is also so much, much more.

Your prophecy was an endowment from Heaven, a gift given to you. It was a transfer from God into your life. In your current battle, I want to tell you that the last word you received from God is the key to your future. Your prophecy is the weapon you need to make your destiny a reality.

Often God prepares us for future struggles with a prophetic word. Sometimes you will receive a prophetic word that doesn't seem to be relevant to your present situation. If that's the case, know that you will need it in the future.

First Timothy 1:18 says, "...*according to the prophecies previously made concerning you, that by them you may wage the good warfare.*" Paul was instructing Timothy to overcome present problems using past prophecies made before the problem came along.

In addition, Paul told Timothy in First Timothy 4:15, "*Meditate on these things; give yourself entirely to them, that your progress may be evident to all.*" Paul was instructing him to meditate, rehearse, and vocalize in his prayer and worship life what had been prophesied to him.

Give yourself to your prophecies. Become completely invested in them. Continually remind yourself of them, pray them aloud, and make them part of your worship.

DON'T SHUT UP, TALK IT UP!

"*O Jerusalem, I have posted watchmen on your walls; **they will pray day and night, continually. Take no rest**, all you who pray to the Lord*" (Isaiah 62:6 NLT). Remember, people who prophetically see the will of God concerning a thing and say it aloud are engaged in prophetic intercession.

Prophetic intercessors are people who seek to know God's will and then pray for it to happen. Did you notice how persistent these people are? The Bible says in Isaiah 62:6, *"They shall never hold their peace day or night...do not keep silent."* They continuously declare the unfinished business of prophetic promises until they are fulfilled.

We constantly remind God of His prophetic promises not because He forgets them but because He is waiting for someone on earth to remember them. Isaiah 62:7 says that we should *"give Him no rest"* until He establishes His prophetic promise on the earth. Press, press, and press God by praying prophetic words He has given you until you see them fulfilled.

IT'S COMING, BUT YOUR EFFORTS ARE REQUIRED

The prophecy you receive is only a potential phenomenon until prayer makes it a present reality.

After three years of famine in Israel, Elijah told the king that rain was coming. How did he know that this was the time for the drought to end and the rain to come? Answer: He heard a prophetic sound. Yes, God can even make a sound prophetic.

First Kings 18:41 says, *"Then Elijah said to Ahab, "Go up, eat and drink; for there is the sound of abundance of rain."* There was no rain yet. So Elijah began to pray.

First Kings 18:42 says, *"So Ahab went up to eat and drink. And Elijah went up to the top of Carmel; then he bowed down on the ground, and put his face between his knees."*

After praying, Elijah sent his servant to see if the sky was cloudy yet. The servant raced outside but returned to report there were no clouds. So Elijah buried his face between his knees again, prayed, and then told his servant to check again. The sky had not changed and there was no indication that it would.

Six times Elijah cried out to God for the fulfillment of a prophetic sound. What, you might ask, did he pray? I'm certain that he prayed the same thing every time: "God, I heard the sound of rain. Please send the rain that I heard to this dry land."

I find it interesting that six prayers weren't enough to bring the miracle. You may know that the number six is the spiritual number for man and that the number seven is the number for the divine. This reminds me that spiritual results are never man-made but always God-made.

The seventh time Elijah prayed and the servant went out to look at the sky, he returned to report that there was a very small cloud in the sky about the size of a man's hand. That was all Elijah needed to hear. He told his servant to warn the king that he had better start going toward home now because a deluge was coming.

The prophetic words God gives you contain all the authority you need to request their fulfillment from God and to command every force standing in the way to get out of the way.

WITHOUT FAITH, PROPHETIC WORDS PERISH

It is impossible to navigate the uncertain prophetic waters of fulfillment without faith. You cannot lay back and say to God, "Well, if that's You, I know You'll do it." Prophecy is a partnership between Heaven and earth, between God and you—and that partnership is established by faith.

Without joining your faith to God's word to you, there is the possibility of shipwreck. Therefore, we cannot automatically discount the prophecy given by a person because a former prophecy didn't come true. There may be a reason for that prophetic failure that is beyond the deliverer of the prophecy. It could be a lack of faith on the part of the receiver of the word.

FAITH REQUIRES A "GOOD CONSCIOUS"

Let's return to our main Scripture for this chapter to discover a faith killer: *"...For some people have deliberately violated their consciences; as a result, their faith has been shipwrecked"* (1 Timothy 1:19 NLT).

You cannot come to God with one issue and not have Him deal with you about other issues that will cause your faith to falter. You cannot claim your prophecy when you have sinful behavior or issues in your life that weaken your faith and affect your conscience. God motivates people who have prophetic faith to work out their issues.

Having a "good conscience" means you are letting God purify you. Letting Him separate you from sins that will weaken your faith, weaken your spiritual discernment, and weaken your walk with God. For example, you can't expect a word about success in your business to come true if you are living in adultery.

Having a good conscience means that to the best of your knowledge you are living out your faith in righteousness to God. It doesn't mean that you are perfect, but it does mean that God can talk to you about anything and you will try to work it out. You might have some stuff you are still struggling with, but you are not hiding or ignoring it and you are believing God for deliverance. If your conscience is not clear with God, you can't have complete faith that God will fulfill a prophetic word.

MAKE WAR WITH YOUR WORD

Make war for the fulfillment of your prophecy by attaching it to your need and directing it toward the mountain that separates you from fulfillment. Use your prophetic word against your adversary, the devil.

When I am praying for someone with a terminal illness, I often give them a word about a future event they are meant to attend. They can then take that word and declare, "I'm going to live and not die and witness this event." They can speak the promise of God through their own prayers and declarations.

Right now, remind yourself of something that God has said to you prophetically; it is time to do some warfare.

- First, thank God for your prophetic word, however you received it.

- Now speak out your prophecy to God.

- Next, speak it to the people who are involved in your word. Call them by name and declare God's will concerning them.

- Then speak to interfering demons and bind them from hindering God's declared will.

- Start prophesying by repeating the word God gave to you.

- Now tell the Lord that you believe your prophetic word by saying, "I believe it, I believe it! I believe it! And I won't give up on the word You have given to me until it comes to pass."

Chapter 6

Prophetic Acts Make Powerful Impacts

What is a prophetic act? I'm glad you asked. It is a physical action directed by the Holy Spirit that supernaturally creates results that change things in our natural world. Prophetic acts activate God's will for a situation. The action in and of itself does not create the change God desires—it triggers God's power to do so. You could say that prophetic acts are God's means to an end.

Sometimes the actions themselves demonstrate a message from God and sometimes not. Prophesying with your actions creates the same results as uttering prophetic words by releasing the will of God into a situation. There are times when God-directed actions really do speak louder than words.

God Is Scrutinizing Your Obstacles

Joshua chapters 5 and 6 tell the story of the children of Israel taking the enemy city of Jericho. God had again parted the waters for them to cross over the Jordan River and enter the Promised Land. Soon after, Joshua was looking down on the city of Jericho, no doubt pondering what would be their best military strategy to conquer this highly fortified city. Probably lost in thought, eventually his awareness returned to the present moment to discover a fierce-looking warrior standing by his side also viewing the walled city.

Understandably startled and probably frightened, Joshua may have put his hand on his sword before asking in a demanding voice, "Are you for us or against us?" Some believe the person Joshua met was Christ or what is called a *Christophany,* "a pre-incarnation manifestation of Christ." Whether it was Christ, the archangel Michael, or some other angelic military commander is not mentioned or important to the story—but what happened next is.

You can almost hear the angel's amusement at the question concerning whose side he was on. His answer was not what Joshua expected: *"Neither one,' he replied…."* That must have surprised Joshua; however, the angel went on to say, *"I am the commander of the Lord's army.' At this, Joshua fell with his face to the ground in reverence…"* (Joshua 5:14 NLT).

The first thing you should notice about this story is that God stands alongside you looking at your situations; He is not far off somewhere in Heaven. He not only understands your dilemma, He cares about the outcome, and He knows your best strategy to solve it. When you are looking at a problem, God is standing right beside you, so turn away from your problems and turn toward Him. Say, "I need Your wisdom to deal with this situation."

In the sixth chapter of Joshua, we discover God's wisdom for the battle of Jericho. It was entirely different from what Joshua would have done or for that matter any other human strategy. He did not tell them to gain entrance by taking a battering ram to the front gate, tunneling under the wall, or using ladders to climb over the walls. Nope. God had a better way for the army of Israel to gain entry into this extremely well-fortified city.

WHEN YOU ACT IN OBEDIENCE, GOD ACTS IN POWER

God's battle strategy was for Joshua to take all two million Israelites and march them around the wall of Jericho once a day for six days without anyone saying a word. Imagine how creepy and confusing this prophetic act must have seemed to the people of Jericho who stood on top of the walls and at their windows watching this silent parade.

I'm sure you noticed that Joshua didn't discuss his suggestions for how to win this battle with the angel. There was no, "In my experience I have found..." or "It seems to me..." or even a "What do you think about this idea...?" No. Joshua shut his mouth and dropped to the ground in worship. Perhaps we should try the same approach with God concerning *our* problems. We would have many more victories if we would just stop talking and start listening to the Lord.

God told Joshua that on the seventh day they were to march around the city seven times. Upon completion of their seventh circuit, the priests were to blow their ram's horns and the people were to give a great shout.

Did you notice that the number of perfection, seven, has shown up again? You should also be aware that they didn't do anything militarily to win the battle until God prepared the way by knocking down the walls.

Consider this: God could have taken the city for them without their effort...but He didn't. Rather, He miraculously created a situation that would allow them to successfully fight their enemy and win. That is the method He normally chooses to help His people with their problems even today. In other words—you should expect to participate in the solution.

The walls of Jericho came down because the people obeyed the command of God. Their prophetic act of marching around the city gave the battle to Israel. When God asks you to do something and you do it, your obedience activates the power He invested in that act.

God's Kingdom on earth is always unleashed in some way when you fulfill a prophetic act.

ANOINTED PROPS

In Second Kings chapter 13, we find prophetic acts in the familiar story of Elisha telling the king of Israel to shoot an arrow out of a window and then to strike the arrows that remained on the ground to ensure victory against his foes.

The first thing you should notice is that, like in the story of the taking of Jericho, God did not require anything expensive or fancy to accomplish His prophetic acts. No holy relics were needed. The props required were just a normal bow and natural arrows; neither of which was in anyway special. They certainly had no anointing upon them until the prophet prophesied and the king executed the prophetic act.

When God tells you to go and get something for a prophetic act...whether it is tangible or intangible...the moment you appropriate it, the prophetic act begins. At that time, the thing becomes anointed to change destiny.

We also have an example of a prophetic act in the New Testament in the person of John the Baptist, cousin of Jesus. John's prophetic act was to look and act like a crazy man. FYI: Although God occasionally asked His Old Testament prophets to do odd things, it was very infrequent. So you can breathe easy, it is very unlikely He would ask something similar of you.

John wore camel hair clothing with a leather belt and his diet was locusts and wild honey. Because of his outfit and diet, no one would ever mistake him for a Pharisee, Sadducee, a priest, rabbi, or any other religious person. Eccentric as he appeared, he was in fact the last of the Old Covenant prophets; Jesus called him the greatest of them, and he had a very special calling.

The point of John the Baptist's prophetic act was to prepare the way for, announce the coming of, and to introduce the Man for whom Israel had waited centuries—their Messiah. In preparation for the Messiah, John called the people of Israel to repentance.

His unusual appearance no doubt reminded them of an earlier prophet, Elijah. John the Baptist's wardrobe is strikingly similar to a description of Elijah found in Second Kings 1:8: *"So they answered him, 'A hairy man wearing a leather belt around his waist.' And he said, 'It is Elijah the Tishbite.'"* John the Baptist was the fulfillment of Malachi 4:5-6 that prophesied Elijah would return to Israel for the Messiah's arrival.

REPURPOSING THE NATURAL

In the story of David and Goliath, found in First Samuel 17:1-51, David used his slingshot to attack the giant. The stone David flung at the giant would have been traveling at about half the speed of a bullet. As a result, the rock didn't kill, but it did knock Goliath down. At that point David could have used any number of things to finish off Goliath. He was holding a slingshot, which he could have used to strangle him, or he could have picked up a rock to bash in his head.

However, David took Goliath's sword to use to exterminate the evil giant and that was a prophetic act. That sword had been used to terrorize thousands and kill hundreds of people. Yet the moment David took it, it became God's sword. When David touched it, the sword that had done so much evil became sanctified to do God's will.

When the Church learns to redeem a cultural tool that has spewed out filth, immorality, or an ungodly cultural agenda—rock music could serve as an example—something prophetically powerful happens.

Like Goliath's sword, things that are used for evil are not evil in themselves. When we repurpose a thing used for evil, it becomes sanctified for spiritual purposes. Redemptive power is unleashed through the act of grabbing and making it our own, whatever it might be.

"SILLY" PROPHETIC ACTS

The story of the healing of Naaman, found in Second Kings 5:8-14, is another example of the power of prophetic acts. When the leprous but wealthy and high-ranking Naaman came to Elisha for healing, he got a big surprise. His expectations for his healing were vastly different from what occurred. When he came to the prophet's house, he expected Elisha to come out, bow before him, perhaps wave his hands over him, maybe chant some odd-sounding words, or possibly require a large financial payment for his healing.

Instead, Elisha did the opposite, refusing to even step outside his house to meet the great man. Rather, Elisha sent his servant out to tell Naaman to wash himself seven times in the River Jordan to obtain his healing. Naaman, an arrogant man of great prestige as the general of an immense army, stormed away furious and insulted. He left in a rage when things didn't go as expected.

In a similar situation we might say, "I thought the man of God would do a Benny Hinn thing over me. I thought I would fall back and a catcher would ease me down. I expected him to put anointing oil on me or perhaps place a prayer cloth on my head. I thought he would do it like they show on TV."

Naaman's counselors tried to talk sense into the angry man but instead he shouted, "We have cleaner rivers than the muddy Jordan in Syria in which to swim." Naaman reasoned that if his healing was only about getting wet, why not do it in clean water. His counselors tried to coax him into doing what the prophet required by saying, "If he would have asked you to do something hard, wouldn't you have done it?" Finally, Naaman got over his indignation enough to be convinced to do as the prophet said. Reluctantly he gave in and went to dip in the Jordan River.

Naaman immersed himself once, came up and looked at his skin and there was no improvement. I believe he may have looked over at his advisors with scorn and thought, *This is the stupidest thing I've ever done.* He went under again, still no change; and he was undoubtedly starting to get angry at those advisors and the prophet.

After the sixth immersion with no results, I suspect he was so angry that he was considering having his counselors and Elisha put into the river to drown. But, he went under those muddy waters one last time and when he came up, the Bible reports in Second Kings 5:14 (NLT), *"...his skin became as healthy as the skin of a young child, and he was healed!"*

MIRACLE-WORKING HANKIES

There is power in prophetic acts even if they seem silly or inappropriate for the desired outcome. However unusual the thing you are directed to do seems, there is power in it.

I believe that some who will read this book, even right now as you are reading, may be only one dip away from a miracle. Could it be you? You may have initiated obedience to do something you thought God wanted you to do, but you didn't see any results and gave up before the finish. It may have been months, years, or even decades and you still haven't seen the results that you believed God would give. I am counseling that you are only one dip away from coming up clean, restored, or possessing what God promised. Don't give up!

> *God gave Paul the power to perform unusual miracles. When handkerchiefs or aprons that had merely touched his skin were placed on sick people, they were healed of their diseases, and evil spirits were expelled* (Acts 19:11-12 NLT).

Have you ever considered how unusual this prophetic act is? Who would think that God's anointing to heal could be captured in a piece of cloth? Taking a handkerchief from an anointed person of God and giving it to a sick person may seem strange and perhaps even a little foolish, but if God told you to do that, it is an anointed prophetic act.

LOST YOUR (AXE) HEAD?

One day the group of prophets came to Elisha and told him, "As you can see, this place where we meet with you is too small" (2 Kings 6:1 NLT).

Consider, could *you* have outgrown the place where *you* are...could God be repositioning *you* to a realm of larger grace, influence, favor, and blessing?

Elisha's prophet trainees in this story went on to say:

"Let's go down to the Jordan River, where there are plenty of logs. There we can build a new place for us to meet." "All right," he told them, "go ahead." "Please come with us," someone suggested. "I will," he said. So he went with them... (2 Kings 6:2-4 NLT).

Things were going well until one of the men dropped his axe head into the water and lost it. He cried out to Elisha for help and Elisha asked him, "Where were you when you last saw it?"

They went to the place where the axe head was lost and Elisha cut a stick and threw it into the water at that very place. Elisha's act made the iron axe head float to the surface so it could be retrieved (2 Kings 6:5-7 NLT).

Okay, everyone knows that iron is too heavy to float and a stick is not magnetic and capable of attracting iron. Elisha's way of retrieving the lost axe head was a prophetic act that overcame the laws of nature.

The way that God is going to give you your miracle is to first take you to the place of your last defeat, the place of your trauma. Elisha took the young prophet back to the place he last saw the axe head.

In the same way, you often have to go back before you can go forward. So, we take the hand of God and He leads us back to where our heart was broken, where our mind was afflicted, where the problem began. If you allow Him, God can take you back there even now.

When we go back to the place where something was lost, God stirs the muddy waters of our dilemma, dredges up what was lost so that we can deal with it, and reattaches the positive elements of that thing to our lives.

END-TIME PROPHETIC ACTS

We are in the last days, and God is moving in a purposeful, forceful, scriptural, prophetic way. His actions are aimed at making the last-days Church all He envisioned it to be. Just as Elisha's prophetic act overcame the laws of nature, so the last-days Church will also frequently circumvent nature's laws through prophetic acts.

When Peter was in prison and the Church prayed, all of a sudden his shackles fell off and the prison doors sprang open and Peter walked out (Acts 12:1-11). Natural law was overcome by Kingdom power.

The Church has to unplug from its mistaken ideal of being "culturally sophisticated" and instead become Kingdom sophisticated, learning and operating in the ways of power in God's Kingdom. Things are about to change as a dynamic power is being unleashed in the last-days Church.

THE TAX MAN COMETH

One day, Peter came to Jesus and said, "We are out of money and they want us to pay taxes." Jesus told Peter to go to the nearest lake, throw out a fishing line, and take the coin out of the mouth of the first fish he caught to pay their debt (see Matthew 17:24-27). Yes, even fishing can be a prophetic act...but only if God wants it to be and never on a Sunday. Get it? That was a joke.

Everything the Church needs it has the authority to appropriate in these last days.

If we don't come to understand that our God is bigger than anything that can happen in our world, we will be shaken every time the stock market collapses, bad news comes along, or adverse politics happen. We need to stop being obsessed with scary things going on in our world and instead become consumed with what is going on in God's unshakable Kingdom. God's power is ready, willing, and able to be released at the right moment to do what He wills for humankind.

BLIND OBEDIENCE

In order for us to be used to release the power and purposes of God on earth through prophetic acts, faith and complete obedience is required. When directed to do a prophetic act, we have to completely fulfill our mission. Incomplete prophetic acts produce incomplete results.

Remember the story earlier in the chapter when the king of Israel was told to shoot an arrow out the window and strike the ground with the remaining arrows? He got part of his prophetic act right, but gave up, striking the ground too soon. He started good but didn't finish well.

His act began in obedience, but a lack of faith caused him to falter. Israel had lost six cities to Syria; and because the king only struck the ground three times, they would only get three of them back. He and all of Israel missed out on God's best due to his lack of faith.

One day as Jesus was headed for Jerusalem the Bible says:

> *...He reached the border between Galilee and Samaria. As he entered a village there, ten men with leprosy stood at a distance, crying out, "Jesus, Master, have mercy on us!" He looked at them and said, "Go show yourselves to the priests." And as they went, they were cleansed of their leprosy* (Luke 17:11-14 NLT).

Had the lepers said, "Well, those priests are all hypocrites, they aren't actually spiritual men. They don't even believe in healing, so why should we show ourselves to them?"and had they followed their own reasoning instead of Jesus' directions, they would not have been healed.

Notice they did not receive their healing while in the temple seeing the priest; they were healed of leprosy *"as they went."* Had they begun to examine and evaluate Jesus' command rather than do it, they would have missed their healing. When their faith was demonstrated by obedience, it was observed by God and He healed them.

Because their faith was complete and their obedience was complete, their healing was also complete.

I want to encourage you to *finish it*. Whatever that statement stirs in your heart right this moment, finish the thing God led you to do. Make your faith in God strong and do the thing God has directed you to do. You could take a step in that direction now.

DITCHES OF DELIGHT

Remember the story mentioned in a previous chapter of Elijah and the two kings of Israel who came to him for a word from God about their war on Moab? Not only did God tell them they would defeat their enemy, He gave them a prophetic act to accomplish that would cause it to happen.

They were to dig ditches throughout the valley so their animals could have water. Without water their animals would be weakened and their enemy would easily overcome them. They did as God directed and in the morning water had miraculously filled their ditches.

This miracle illustrates what we all know but often forget, God is always one step ahead of us. God was going to send water to them, but they had to be ready for it. Hence, He told them to dig ditches. By completing their prophetic act, they were able to capture the blessing God was sending them.

Imagine how crazy it must have seemed to those soldiers to dig ditches when there was no lake or streams to supply water to fill them. What happened was this: it rained in the land they came from and the water flowed from their *past* location into the valley where they were currently located to meet *present* need.

In the same way, God can bring something from your past life into your present life to meet your current needs.

However, water for their animals wasn't the only reason for the ditches. When the enemy came the next day, looked down on the valley and saw the ditches filled with water, the water appeared to them to be blood. Thinking that their enemy had already been destroyed, they came casually into the valley planning to plunder what they thought were dead men. The armies of Israel easily overwhelmed these unsuspecting soldiers. Israel's obedience to a prophetic act brought the hand of God for a great victory (see 2 Kings 3:1-24).

Even when obeying God may seem like you are doing something that is small and unimportant, remember that God doesn't have any "small and unimportant acts." No matter how strange or inconsequential it may appear, if that prophetic act is important enough for God's Spirit to lead you to do it, then it is certainly important enough for you to do.

If you've had the impulse to help someone in need, it may have been more than just a moment of pity and may have been a leading of God to give them some money or help them in some way. You might have talked yourself out of a directive from God by thinking that they would squander what you gave them.

When we obey the leading of the Holy Spirit, although the reason may seem obscure or irrelevant, power is unleashed by our obedience.

Should God ask you to give five bucks in the offering and you did it, it is the same to God as if you gave five million dollars. Do you see it? God values your obedience above all else. Your actions based on a specific request from God releases power into your life.

The next time you *feel* like you should do something generous, just do it. Even should you be mistaken, God will honor and reward you for your desire to be obedient and helpful.

Know that there are consequences for obedience and also consequences for disobedience for what God asks us to do. When we learn to be good stewards of Kingdom commands and do the prophetic acts we are given, we will have the awesome opportunity to participate in the miracles God is performing in our day.

Chapter 7

A GUIDE TO PROPHETIC HEALING

The potency of the prophetic is the power behind the punch of the Church—and the atmosphere it creates can bring God's Kingdom to earth.

Everyone is supposed to pray for the sick, and I'll prove that statement in a minute. Hopefully we've already established that every Christian should be prophetic and hear from God, or at least you are considering it. This chapter then is about how your ability to hear and your ability to heal connect when God gives you an opportunity to minister to others.

When the Church gets to the place where most believers can access God's power through the Holy Spirit, we will change the world.

Do you consider yourself "one of those who believe"? If yes, let's take a look at how Jesus describes you:

> *And these signs will follow **those who believe: In My name they will cast out demons;** they will **speak with new tongues;** they will take up serpents; and if they drink anything deadly, it will by no means hurt them; **they will lay hands on the sick, and they will recover*** (Mark 16:17-18).

Well, that Scripture makes it pretty clear that you, along with all Christians, are called to prophetic healing.

WHERE THE PROPHETIC MEETS THE DEMONIC

Jesus was able to discern the origins of the diseases of the people He healed. He knew if their disease came from the demonic or had another cause.

The more sophisticated the Church has become, the less we admit there is a devil or even that there is evil in the world. If you were to visit most evangelical churches, it is unlikely that you would get the slightest hint that the world we live in is under the influence of the demonic. It is hard to defeat an enemy you don't believe in. Yet the New Testament clearly states:

> *Our struggle is not against blood and flesh,*
> *but against the rulers, against the powers,*
> *against* **the world forces of this darkness**,
> *against* **the spiritual forces of wicked-**
> **ness** *in the heavenly places* (Ephesians 6:12
> NASB).

During my senior year in high school, I learned a lesson that I'll never forget. The two biggest football players were blindfolded with pillowcases and then had a pillow fight with each other. Then unbeknown to one guy, the blindfold was removed from the other guy, and the pillow fight continued.

As you would expect, the guy who could see pounded the blinded guy time after time and was clearly the winner. The blindfolded guy lost dramatically for the sole reason that he was blind to the actions of his enemy. Likewise, we in the Church cannot be blind to the spiritual world around us and expect to do our job and fulfill our purpose.

Jesus, our example in all things, when healing people would often first deal with the evil spirit involved in their illness if there was one. Should an evil spirit be present in a person, obviously, it would be responsible for the person's infirmity. At least half of the times Jesus healed someone, He first commanded an unclean spirit to come out; however, it was not every time.

In the charismatic church, we like to make everything into an easy-to-use formula. Some people cast out demons every time they pray for a person's healing. It may have worked a few times, so they use the cast-the-demon-out formula every time they pray for healing. But there is a problem with that. Jesus didn't always do it that way.

My dad pastored a church during the mid-sixties that ministered to hippies. In our hippie church we often dealt with drug demons. However, we also dealt with caffeine demons, and my personal favorite, the Coca-Cola demon. People with that demon couldn't break their Coca-Cola addiction. Okay, the part about the caffeine and Coca-Cola demons is, of course, a joke to illustrate how easy it is to blame every problem on demons.

DON'T PET THE DEMONS

When Jesus discerned that an evil spirit was involved in a person's health problem, He would rebuke it. Therefore, to minister as Jesus did, we have to stop ignoring the demonic world and be willing to take it on. However, when ministering prophetically to people who have a health problem related to the demonic, we must always show the person kindness and love.

Never speak harshly to people whose health issues are due to the demonic—and never talk lovingly to demons. Don't placate demons and don't rebuke people.

When God shows me that a person's sickness has a demonic origin, I handle it like this: I first reassure the person that Jesus loves and is for him or her. Then I ask permission to deal with the infirmity. That is, when I speak powerfully to any demonic presence causing the problem, I might say something like, "Demon, come out of this person!" Then when I'm finished praying against that demonic presence, I reassure the person again that God loves him or her very much.

The next thing to do is to help the person determine how the demon gained access so that steps for protection can be made to prevent it from happening again.

If fear of offending someone keeps you from dealing with the person's demonic problem, consider this. Shouldn't you be more concerned about what will happen if you don't deal with it? When I recognize the devil's presence, I must do something about it.

SPIRIT-EMPOWERED PRAYERS

Jesus was always sensitive to the leading of the Spirit of God. So before you pray for someone's healing, breathe a prayer and ask the Holy Spirit how to pray. When you allow God to lead, you will have good results.

Following is what happened when Jesus encountered the very unusual condition of a man who was unable to speak. Who would think that the inability to speak could be caused by a demon? Jesus, however, listened to the Holy Spirit and knew exactly how to handle the situation:

> *When they left, a demon-possessed man who couldn't speak was brought to Jesus. So Jesus cast out the demon, and then the man began to speak. The crowds were amazed. "Nothing like this has ever happened in Israel!" they exclaimed* (Matthew 9:32-33 NLT).

In this case, Jesus had to cast out a demon to heal the man. However, Jesus healed many times when there was no need to cast out demons. Hence, we must understand that the root cause of sickness can be demonic but it can also have another source.

In speaking of demons, Jesus teaches in Luke 11:21-22 (NLT):

> *For when a strong man is fully armed and guards his palace, his possessions are safe— until someone even stronger attacks and overpowers him, strips him of his weapons, and carries off his belongings.*

If a problem is caused by a demon, you won't have lasting results until you oust the *"strong man,"* the demon causing the problem. In the same vein, the Church can't take cities for Christ until they first acknowledge and deal with the demonic principality over that city. Also, if you speak with people who seem hardened in their heart and unable to hear the Gospel, it is often due to the interference of a demonic spirit that must be prayed off of them.

WE ARE "THEY"

When you pray for the sick, the Lord may reveal certain facts about the origins of the disease in order to build faith and give encouragement to the sick person. That information is also intended to give the ministering person the knowledge they need to bring about lasting results.

When I pray for people, I sometimes see things that happened in their past that are at the root of their problem. When I speak out loud what God has shown me, I can feel people's faith surge. That surge tremendously increases the chances for healing to result.

If we want to minister to the sick, it is vital that we allow God to give us a discerning heart so we can know how and what to pray.

Lest you think moving in this realm is too scary or too difficult for you, let me remind you again of the description Jesus gave of a born-again person, which is found in Mark 16:17: *"…In My name they will cast out demons…."* We are the *"they."*

THE DEVIL IS A CHEATER

When I was a young assistant pastor, a couple who had recently been born again came to me with a problem. The man was a professor at the University of South Carolina and his wife was a medical professional. They told me that things had started moving around in their house and they were concerned that the house was haunted.

They said that when having dinner, sometimes things would fall to the floor for no apparent reason or even slide across the room. They asked me what they should do. I told them that I would come to their home and show them how to fix this problem.

I went to their house, walked in the front door, and shouted, "Devil, OUT!" and pointed to the door. The demonic presence left. They asked me if that was all they needed to do. "Yes," I said and told them that demons have no right to enter the home of believers and harass them. Also, I pointed out that if a person twenty-two years old could get rid of a demon, they could certainly do the same.

You don't need a special ceremony, holy water, or some kind of ancient incantation to toss the devil out on his ear.

The actions of this demon were illegal. The devil has no right to be within the homes of born-again people. The only reason he had been successful was because the devil cheated, and they didn't know their rights and how to enforce them.

If the devil has ever awakened you with a nightmare, you should get really mad at him because he cheated and doesn't have a right to do that to a born-again person. He has broken a boundary and you must rebuke and cast him away.

REVEAL IT AND GOD WILL HEAL IT

In Jesus' day, people could not enter the temple if they had any kind of illness or infirmity. So people would hide their physical problems to gain access. Everyone knew they had a problem, but no one wanted to talk about it. Consequently, they were reluctant to disclose their issues to each other and to God.

In our day, we do something similar. When people come to church we expect them to be happy and perfect. It is as if we pass out fake smiles—"Don't forget the pastor likes everyone smiling and remember to turn your smile in on your way out." I am proud that my church is a safe place for people to admit they have a need or an issue and know that they are welcome.

Mark chapter 3 tells of the day when Jesus showed up at the temple with His "issue detector" turned on. By the Holy Spirit, Jesus was made aware of a man attending church that day with a withered, or we would call it a deformed, hand. So Jesus said to the man whose deformed hand was hidden, "Stretch forth your hand."

When Jesus told the man with the deformity to "Show your hand," He was saying, "You reveal it and I'll heal it." I almost never exercise any aspect of prophetic ministry without having the opportunity to tie it into some form of healing. God wants to heal every kind of problem people have, whether mental, spiritual, or physical.

Disease can become entrenched in a person's identity. When you are sick for a long period of time, your infirmity begins to define you. You and the people around you begin to label and identify you by your affliction.

It often takes a supernatural exercise of the Kingdom to dislodge an infirmity that has had a long-term presence in someone's life. This is an aspect of healing we might never recognize in a person unless we allow the Holy Spirit to guide us in our prayers for the sick.

THE PROPHETIC UNCOVERS ROOT CAUSES

John 5 tells of Christ healing the man at the Pool of Bethesda. Later at the temple Jesus gave the man an unusual prophetic word about his healing and the possibility of a future illness:

Afterward Jesus found him in the temple, and said to him, "See, you have been made well. Sin no more, lest a worse thing come upon you" (John 5:14).

Apparently, the man's condition was due to sinful behavior in his early life. Jesus was telling him to not open the door to sickness again by sinning. He discerned that the illness did not come from a demonic source but had a sin origin.

We must have a clear understanding from the Holy Spirit concerning a person's illness before we pray, so that we can help the person overcome it now and in the future. When we are blind to the nature of the battle with satan and sin, we are merely swinging at the air like my blinded friend in the high school pillow fight.

In Second Kings 2:19, we find the beginning of an interesting story: *"Then the men of the city said to Elisha, 'Please notice, the situation of this city is pleasant, as my lord sees; but the water is bad, and the ground barren.'"*

Elisha responded:

"Bring me a new bowl with salt in it." So they brought it to him. Then he went out to the spring that supplied the town with water and threw the salt into it. And he said, "This is what the Lord says: I have purified this

water. It will no longer cause death or infertility" (2 Kings 2:20-21 NLT).

Notice that Elisha went to the *source* of the bad water, the spring. If the source of an issue is not discerned and dealt with, then you can expect the problem to reoccur.

God's love can be like a healing potion; and many times when we pray for people, God will give them a deeper revelation of His love. His love then goes to the source of their problem and heals them.

WORDS WITH WINGS

I mentioned this before but I want to remind you that in prophetic healing when you hear something from God about the infirmity and repeat it to people, their faith is built up for their healing.

Healing can be sent to the sick by an anointed prophetic declaration. You don't have to be present to pray for the sick. My favorite Scripture confirming this truth is Psalm 107:20 (NLT), "*He sent out his word and healed them, snatching them from the door of death.*" After praying with someone for friends or family members living in another city, I often hear reports of their healing.

There are no boundaries for God's Word; it works here, there, and everywhere on earth. In Matthew 8:8, a Centurion came to Jesus for the healing of his servant. Jesus told him that He would go with him to his house, but the Centurion said that was unnecessary: *"...But only speak a word, and my servant will be healed."* As those who minister prophetically, we can discern, speak, and declare things for people who are not present with us.

It is amazing what God can do when we break free from the limits our minds place on Him.

Prophetic Wisdom for a Natural Remedy

In First Kings 20, we find the story of King Hezekiah of Israel who was dying. The prophet Isaiah came to the home of the king and told him to get his affairs in order because he would soon be gone. When the king heard that his death was imminent, he wept and cried out to God for healing. Isaiah hadn't even departed the courtyard of Hezekiah's residence before God told him to return to the king with a different word. Isaiah then prophesied to Hezekiah that he would be healed and his life would be extended for fifteen years.

The following is the unusual means by which God chose to heal Hezekiah: *"Then Isaiah said, 'Make an ointment from figs.' So Hezekiah's servants spread the ointment over the boil, and Hezekiah recovered!"* (2 Kings 20:7 NLT). Although there was a supernatural aspect to this healing, God also used a natural element.

Several years ago, I was heading to Newport Beach, California, to speak in a Sunday evening service. I had a lump on my head, so before I left Phoenix, my wife put her hands on me and prayed. She said, "I curse that thing and command it to leave." I thought it would just fall off, but God had a very different plan.

After the service in Newport Beach that evening, a lady who was a surgeon came up to me. She said, "Sorry, I didn't hear a word you said because I couldn't take my eyes off the big lump on your head." She went on to say that she would not be able to sleep tonight unless she took care of the bump for me.

She invited me to come to her office that evening as soon as I was free. When I asked if she was certain that she wanted to do this, she was adamant. It was as if she was driven to take care of my lump. As I drove to her office I thought, *Could this be the miracle my wife and I prayed for?*

Upon arriving at her office, she did a quick and simple procedure that took care of the lump.

When I awoke the next morning lump-free, I thought, *I didn't expect my healing to happen this way but…cool. Free midnight surgery at Newport Beach, who would have thought?* Yes, God can and will use doctors, medicine, and natural remedies to heal His people.

Sometimes the solution to a problem is treatable chemically, through nutrition, changes in the diet, or with a lifestyle adjustment. We still believe in supernatural miracles; but there is certainly nothing wrong with God steering us to a natural remedy.

YOU CAN BE A PROPHETIC PHYSICIAN

Are you willing to tell the Lord that you want to be used in prophetic healing? Our world is hurting and in need of healing, and I'm convinced that to meet the need we should follow in Jesus' footsteps. Everywhere He went He not only preached the coming of the Kingdom, He also *healed the sick*—and we need to do the same.

If you will surrender to God to be used by Him in this way, He will definitely use you. There are many more sick people in our world than there are practicing prophetic physicians to help them. So, God needs *you*, and you, as a believer, are called to do this!

By bringing healing to the hurting, we are demonstrating God's love in a tangible way.

When you feel God pulling on your compassion for someone, the reason is often to bring prophetic healing to the person. You might be thinking, *But Pastor, I don't know how to do these things*. If this was something you had to do out of your own power and ability, I might agree. But you don't have to worry about the "'how to." This is all you need to do:

1. Relax in your faith in God's goodness, love, and care for you—speak your gratitude to Him.

2. Open yourself to permitting God's love to flow through you—tell the Lord that you desire to be used to express His love.

3. The Holy Spirit is standing next to you for the purpose of guiding you— ask for His help and direction.

4. Go to the person who needs prophetic healing—tell the person how much God loves and wants to heal him or her. Speak healing to the person as the Spirit leads you.

What an incredible honor God would bestow upon us. He would give us His healing grace so that through it we can make His love known to a suffering world.

Chapter 8

THE PROPHETIC PREVAILS OVER JEZEBEL

Jezebel symbolizes the essence of the spirit of witchcraft; this spirit that operates in both men and women to control others through manipulation, intimidation, and domination.

Some have described the Jezebel spirit in a way that demeans women, but this spirit is not associated with any particular gender. I have met as many, if not more, male Jezebels than female ones. Those who use witchcraft knowingly access the satanic realm for their purposes. However, not all who operate in the Jezebel spirit realize that what they are doing is demonic.

PROPHETIC PEOPLE SCARE THE DEVIL

The Bible gives us insight into the thing Jezebel feared the most in First Kings 18:4 (NLT): *"…Jezebel had tried to kill all the Lord's prophets…."* Jezebel, the sorceress wife of Ahab, king of Israel, knew that her greatest opponent was the voice of God to His people through the prophets. Hence, she waged war against her archenemy, the prophetic.

Sometimes you can discover how important something spiritual is by how severely it is dealt with by the devil.

When the devil attacks you, you might think that you aren't important enough or what you are doing isn't world transforming enough to merit the devil's attention. However, you need to realize that the devil's attacks may not be solely about what you are doing today. It may be about something he sees in your future. Sometimes the enemy has a better sense of what God has in store for us than we do.

WITCH'S PAWN

First Kings 21:25 (NLT) tells us of the danger of submitting to the spirit of Jezebel: *"No one else so completely sold himself to what was evil in the Lord's sight as Ahab did under the influence of his wife Jezebel.*" Jezebel completely controlled her spineless husband. When a weak person is in a place of authority, the controlling person will always usurp the power.

Scripture confirms that Jezebel was in fact a witch in the following conversation between her son, Joram, and the man who would replace him as king. When Joram asked Jehu if he had come in peace, "*Jehu replied, 'How can there be peace as long as the idolatry and witchcraft of your mother, Jezebel, are all around us?'*" (2 Kings 9:22 NLT).

REBELLION GIVES BIRTH TO WITCHCRAFT

After King Saul had disobeyed instructions given by the Lord, he tried to justify himself by offering sacrifices. The response of Samuel, the prophet to Saul's sin, gives us a clearer understanding of the foundation of witchcraft. First Samuel 15:22-23 (NLT) says:

> *…What is more pleasing to the Lord: your burnt offerings and sacrifices or your obedience to his voice? Listen!* **Obedience is better than sacrifice, and submission is better than offering the fat of rams. Rebellion is as sinful as witchcraft**, *and stubbornness as bad as worshiping idols. So because you have*

rejected the command of the Lord, he has rejected you as king.

Before we go on talking about the Jezebel spirit, I want to point out a vitally important truth found in this Scripture—you can't buy back through sacrifice what you lose through disobedience. A more modern application might be, you can't buy forgiveness from God for your sin of Saturday night with a check in the offering on Sunday.

Doing something right doesn't negate the sin of doing something wrong. Only genuine repentance and turning away from that sin brings forgiveness.

This Scripture also tells us that witchcraft is a form of rebellion, rebellion against God and His authority. When we talk about witchcraft, people usually think about witches, warlock, séances, curses, the black arts, and satanists. Yes, that is certainly a sphere of witchcraft, and the people who take part in those things were seduced into it by the promise of getting the ability to control others. They are open about their rebellion against God. However, many people who operate in the spirit of Jezebel hide their allegiance to the devil and some are even unaware of it.

You might be surprised to learn that there is more witchcraft of the Jezebel variety within the Church than outside its doors. The "religious spirit" is a brother to the spirit of Jezebel because it too seeks to control the actions of others. Even though people operating in a religious spirit may attend church every time the doors are open and disguise themselves with hyper-religious behavior, nevertheless, they are in rebellion against God.

WITCHCRAFT IS A DESIRE OF THE SINFUL NATURE

Witchcraft occurs when we give in to the temptation of our flesh to control others through manipulation, intimidation, and domination. The Bible calls witchcraft or sorcery a desire of the sinful nature in Galatians 5:19-21 (NLT):

> *When you follow the **desires of your sinful nature**, the results are very clear: sexual immorality, impurity, lustful pleasures, idolatry, **sorcery**, hostility, quarreling, jealousy, outbursts of anger, selfish ambition, dissension, division, envy, drunkenness, wild parties, and other sins like these. ...anyone living that sort of life will not inherit the Kingdom of God.*

You may have someone in your family or know a person who could be described by the word "manipulative." Sometimes these people may use emotions, tears, and anger to control you. They might even manufacture a crisis to get your full attention. Perhaps you dismissed their actions as, "Just the way they are." However, it is more than that; it really is witchcraft.

We can operate in the Jezebel spirit without realizing how serious and how sinful being manipulative is.

CONTROL FREAK

Everyone can be tempted to try to control others; and if we have a position of authority, the temptation is even stronger. As parents, we are expected to teach our children right and wrong, but we must be very careful to never take the place of the authority that belongs to God in another's life, even our children. Many times our job, instead of being controlling, is to take the person's hand and offer it to God.

That means that we are not going to tell our adult children and those we have influence over who to marry, where to work, and how to live their lives. Instead, we are going to encourage them to go to God for the answers to these very important life issues.

Some people who claim to be prophets in our day may actually be control freaks with a prophetic gift. They may even think that by using their gift along with their controlling spirit they gain status with God. However, it isn't your gift but your character that gives you merit in God's eyes.

Jezebel knew how to manipulate men through seduction. When a woman uses sex to get her way or to manipulate a man in some way, it is witchcraft. Seduction is one way to control others; however, there are thousands of other ways to be manipulative.

All of us at one time or another have done a little witchcraft according to its biblical definition of being controlling. Everyone is guilty of usurping the rightful place of God in a person's life by exercising more control over someone than we should.

ANY SIN CAN BECOME DEMONIZED

When we begin to be a controlling influence over someone's life through fear, flattery, intimidation, domination, manipulations, etc., suddenly we are no longer alone. Unbeknown to us, a spirit can join in our controlling activities and what began in the flesh then becomes demonized. It begins as a simple temptation to control others; but as we continue to exercise that fleshly desire, it becomes much more.

In fact, all sins of the flesh can become demonized. Initially, we can control whether we commit a certain sin or not. However, if we continue to practice that sin, eventually it will become something beyond our control. By repeating a sin, we create an opening to a demonic influence.

For example, a person can be tempted by pornography and occasionally give in to it. However, when it becomes a regular occurrence, the person loses the ability to stop sinning in that way. The enemy has gained entrance through that sin and now the person is chained to it.

It doesn't matter how spiritual you believe you are, when you continually give in to a sin of the flesh, it will eventually become demonized and uncontrollable.

JEZEBEL'S WEAPON WAS WORDS

First Kings chapter 18 tells of a contest of spiritual power that took place at Mount Carmel between Elijah and 450 prophets of Baal and the 400 prophets of Asherah who were Jezebel's favorites. All the children of Israel showed up to watch the face-off between the God of Elijah and the fake gods, Baal and Asherah.

All 950 false prophets tried everything they could think of all day long to call down fire from Heaven to ignite their sacrifice, but nothing happened. Finally, Elijah said enough is enough and he drenched his sacrifice in water, called down fire from God, and the sacrifice was consumed. In that moment, Elijah turned the heart of a nation to God.

We also must learn how to contend with the spirit of Jezebel to advance God's Kingdom on earth.

Then Elijah killed all 950 pagan prophets and Ahab went back to the palace and told Jezebel what Elijah had done. Jezebel was very angry and sent Elijah a message. She sent him "words" saying that he would be a dead man in twenty-four hours.

Her words carried a curse that became a nightmare vision for Elijah, and his world darkened. Even after defeating the 950 pagan priests, he ran away from one woman in fear. Yes, Jezebel used words to cast a spell upon Elijah. The oppression of witchcraft came to him through her words.

Elijah was so affected by the witch's words that he ran for two days to escape what he believed to be his imminent death. Finally, he sat exhausted under a tree, prayed that he might die, and then passed out. The rest of the story, in short, is that God sent angels to save his life. Elijah then went to Mount Horeb and reconnected with God who restored him and gave him a plan that would end the rule of witchcraft over Israel. (See First Kings 19.)

HOW TO KNOW IF YOU ARE BEING ATTACKED BY WITCHCRAFT

There are four things in the preceding story that helps us recognize if we are being attacked by witchcraft:

1. Elijah experienced fear, anxiety, stress, and exhaustion; he was stressed out, filled with panic, and physically fatigued far more than he should have been from a mere threat.

2. His second day on the run, Elijah left his trusted servant and wanted to be alone. Isolation is unhealthy and the desire for it isn't normal.

3. He was despondent, demoralized, disappointed, and depressed. When Elijah killed the pagan priests, he thought that he had won the victory once and for all, but he was mistaken. The very spirit he had triumphed over one day came after him the following day. The real problem in Israel wasn't the 950 false prophets; it was the demonic Jezebel spirit and the witch behind it. It is my belief that depression, most of the time, has a spiritual source and is in some way a manifestation of witchcraft.

4. Elijah had self-destructive or suicidal thoughts. He was probably thinking, *What's the use; I've failed God and*

myself. A spiritually healthy person doesn't have those thoughts. These thoughts are not merely the symptoms of a melancholy moment but of a demonic attack.

YOUR WORDS HAVE POWER TOO

When I first became pastor of Eagle's Nest Church, there was a time when I was unusually depressed for two weeks. During that time, I asked God's forgiveness for my sins and for the sins of everyone I could think of. Finally, I heard from God and He informed me, "Words have been spoken against you."

I was in the Spirit as soon as He spoke and I saw the pulpits at two churches where I had served as an assistant pastor. As I watched, both pastors cursed me from their pulpits. They declared to their congregations, "He will fail in Arizona because God is not with him."

Over the next two weeks, I had visitors from both churches who confirmed my vision. They told me that their pastors said I was out of God's will and would fail. As I considered what had happened, I was stunned and couldn't believe a man of God would or could have the ability to curse me. The truth, however, was that though they were "men of God," they both had uncontrolled tongues and unresolved emotional issues. Instead of blessing their spiritual son, they actually put a curse on me.

The enemy has a gun—and we can provide him bullets with our words. When those pastors spoke failure over me, they loaded the enemy's gun and he began stalking me.

I asked God what I was supposed to do. The Lord took me to Luke 6:28 (NLT), which clearly says what God expects of us when we are cursed, *"Bless those who curse you. Pray for those who hurt you."* I've learned to never worry about the person who curses me; rather, I choose to address their words and the demonic spirit using them.

The prophetic anointing is greater than and has authority over the spirit of Jezebel.

While walking through my spiritual education, God gave me a Scripture that explains how to combat witchcraft:

> *"No weapon formed against you shall prosper,*
> *and **every tongue** [word] **which rises against***
> ***you in judgment you shall condemn**. This is*
> *the heritage of the servants of the Lord, and*
> *their righteousness is from Me," says the Lord*
> (Isaiah 54:17).

What is your most effective weapon against witchcraft and the Jezebel spirit? Your WORDS! Your defense against words spoken against you is your words that "condemn" and rebuke them.

So, I declared, "I break every word spoken against my life! I cancel those words even though they were spoken by godly men." It really didn't matter who declared the words that cursed me. Whether it was a satanist standing on a mountain in front of an altar or a preacher standing behind a pulpit, the results were the same. Because those pastors stood in places of spiritual authority, the words they spoke had a spiritual impact and mobilized hell.

Words themselves contain no power—until they become weaponized by either Heaven or hell.

CREATE A NO-CURSING ZONE

Some people are still being governed by the words of dead people. For example, your father in anger may have declared that you were "lazy," "stupid," or some other derogatory thing. Although he may be dead, his assertions about you may still control you as if you were a puppet on a string. Despite those words, you don't have to live that way any longer, you can be free!

Our prophetic defense against curses is based on the fundamental truth that words spoken by a higher power overrule those spoken by a lesser power. Words from God's mouth or God's words spoken by His people have authority over every word uttered by the devil, demons, Jezebels, or the people influenced by them.

Now, turn all this around and apply it to yourself. Do you want to have *your words* used by satan to cause

WHAT *is* HEAVEN SAYING?

someone's downfall? Of course you don't. So, when you become upset, do not allow yourself to curse your spouse, your children, other family members, friends, your pastor, your president, or any person you find offensive. The Scripture is very clear about the kinds of words we should speak:

> *Let no corrupt word proceed out of your mouth, but what is good for necessary edification, that it may impart grace to the hearers* (Ephesians 4:29).

> *With it* [our mouth] *we bless our God and Father, and with it we curse men, who have been made in the similitude of God. Out of the same mouth proceed blessing and cursing. My brethren, these things ought not to be so* (James 3:9-10).

THE AGE OF AQUARIUS

There are those who would create a counterfeit of God's Kingdom on earth. They seek to build a community of harmony, world peace, social justice, and economic equality. Who wouldn't want that? Because this sounds so good it is tempting to many, even to many Christians. However, this is a fantasy based on the devil's deception that we can eliminate evil and have Heaven on earth without Christ. A kingdom built on humanism rather than God.

Just as the name implies, humanism is all about humans and nothing about God. There is no place for God in this philosophy. In fact, humanists see religion as evil and a roadblock to establishing their version of the Garden of Eden.

The Church needs to recognize what is going on and realize the opposition it faces due to the persuasive preaching of this message around the world in colleges and universities and throughout the media.

When someone tries to force something to happen that only God can accomplish, they will always resort to the power of witchcraft.

God's Son gave His life to establish His Kingdom on the earth. Christians are called to play a part in bringing it about, but only Jesus can complete it. Those who have been deceived by this anti-Christ doctrine will use words empowered by witchcraft and every means possible to try to establish this New Age. What they are actually trying to create is satan's kingdom on earth.

We know how this story will end, but each of us have a job to do to bring God's Kingdom to earth. The glorious day is coming that is described in Habakkuk 2:14, *"For the earth will be filled with the knowledge of the glory of the Lord, as the waters cover the sea."*

PEACEFUL COEXISTENCE WITH JEZEBEL? NO WAY!

In Second Kings 9, we have the story of the end of Jezebel and her family. Elisha sent a young prophet with a flask of oil to a godly man named Jehu. He was a military commander, a man of some consequence and distinction. At his meeting with Jehu, the young prophet poured oil over his head, declared him to be king, and charged him with the job of killing the witch Jezebel and her family.

Jehu immediately attacked Jezebel's son, Joram, who had become king of Israel following his brother's and father's death. After taking out Joram, it was time to move against Jezebel, so Jehu went to Jezebel's home in Jezreel. When Jezebel heard that Jehu was in town, *"she painted her eyelids and fixed her hair"*—in other words, she made herself seductive (2 Kings 9:30 NLT).

When Jezebel looked out her window and saw Jehu, she no doubt fluttered her eyes while asking if he had come in peace. I believe that she had never met a man she couldn't seduce and manipulate. Jehu apparently was immune to her wiles and his answer was a firm "No," that he had not come in peace.

There is an important point here: God's plan for Israel's good was not to make peace with Jezebel. You cannot make peace with a Jezebel spirit. If you try to placate a person using this spirit, you will lose more ground than you take.

Because sometimes we don't want to fight and desire peace, we can be tempted to give in to this spirit and hope for peaceful coexistence. However, there can be no peace with the Jezebel spirit because it always wants to control everything and everyone.

Anything the devil gives you he can always take back, and sooner or later he will.

JEZEBEL'S TURN TO FEED THE DOGS

Back to the story of the defeat of Jezebel. Jehu looked up at the window where Jezebel stood. Then, because he had an anointing to bring this woman down, Jehu shouted, "Who's on my side?" Out of adjoining windows, two or three eunuchs were looking out at him.

Eunuchs, as you know, are men who were castrated against their will so they could be trusted around women of royal blood. They often symbolize angels because they were without sex.

When Jehu saw them, he commanded them, "Throw her down!" and they did. This almost sounds too easy but it was only possible because a man anointed for the job followed God's plan.

After Jezebel fell to her death in the streets, the prophecy concerning her demise was fulfilled by the end of the day: *"And regarding Jezebel, the Lord says, 'Dogs will eat Jezebel's body at the plot of land in Jezreel'"* (1 Kings 21:23 NLT).

CHARISMATIC WITCHCRAFT

One Sunday, I was to preach at a church in California. Upon arrival at the airport, the pastor picked me up. It was three hours until service time and I was exhausted. I asked him to take me to my hotel so that I could rest and pray before the service. He begrudgingly did so. I lay down and immediately went to sleep, but soon after I was awakened by a slap across my face. Shocked because I had never experienced anything like that before, I immediately dropped to my knees and began praying in the Spirit.

Soon the Lord showed me a vision of the pastor as he drove away from my hotel after dropping me off. While driving home he said, "Damn that lazy preacher." Then I watched as a demon with a big smile on his face flew over to me laughing and slapped my face.

The pastor had spiritual jurisdiction in that city and that part of the Kingdom; and because of that, his words had power.

The Lord spoke to me and said, "Never damn someone unless I tell you to." As Proverbs 18:21 says, *"Death and life are in the power of the tongue...."*

Are you wondering what I did when the pastor picked me up for church? Did I tell him what a jerk he was and what he had done to me? No, I preached that night and never mentioned my odd experience to the pastor.

That happened when I was a young man and God has taught me so much since then: I've learned that love always wins and forgiveness disarms the assignments of the devil. I also learned that witchcraft and the Jezebel spirit will not go away on its own. Somebody in the Kingdom has to put a stop to it.

NOW IT'S YOUR TURN

Are you ready to do a little warfare on your own behalf? I've repeated the list of things that indicate if you are under spiritual attack. Look at it again and determine if any of it applies to you.

1. Have you experienced an unusual amount of fear, anxiety, stress or exhaustion, panic, or are you physically fatigued more than normal?

2. Have you felt abnormally isolated?

3. Are you unusually despondent, demoralized, and depressed?

4. Do you feel surrounded by a dark world; are you experiencing self-destructive or

suicidal thoughts and wonder if there is
a reason to go on living?

If you have one or more of these symptoms, we need to take action against it now. Or, if you feel that your father or anyone else has intentionally or accidentally placed a word curse on you, then the following is also for you.

If we were in the same room and you were standing before me, I would pray for you. However, there is nothing I can do that you cannot do for yourself.

You don't have to trace back to where this thing came from, you can just break it off and be free.

Are you ready? I want you to speak aloud the verse found in Isaiah 54:17:

> *"No weapon formed against you shall prosper, and every tongue which rises against you in judgment you shall condemn. This is the heritage of the servants of the Lord, And their righteousness is from Me," says the Lord.*

Memorize it and make it part of your prayer life for the next several days or weeks. Use it as needed to combat any symptoms of a curse that tries to reemerge. You can expect the devil to fight you over your declaration, but don't give up. You have to show the enemy that you are determined to be free and that you will fight him with God's Word for as long as it takes.

PRAY WITH ME

Pray right now aloud:

Father God, I worship and praise You. I commit my life to You, all of my life. I ask Your forgiveness for any sins of omission or commission. Forgive me for having wrong attitudes. Forgive me for speaking wrong words. Forgive me for doing wrong things.

I thank You for the forgiveness available to me through the blood of Jesus. Thank You for washing me clean in the precious blood of Your Son and redeeming me from the enemy and transferring me out of darkness into Your Kingdom of light. I thank You, Lord, for Your Spirit, Your Son, Your Kingdom, and Your Word.

Now in Jesus' name, I boldly stand upon Your Word and declare over my life that: No weapon formed against me shall prosper and every word spoken against me I cancel, condemn, rebuke, and destroy in Jesus' name.

Devil, you are a liar! You have NO authority over me. I take the authority given to me by God over the spirit of Jezebel and over all witchcraft and declare that every curse is now broken.

*Lord, I am Yours; have Your way in my life.
May Your Kingdom come and Your will be
done on earth and in me as it is in Heaven.
In Jesus' mighty name I pray, amen.*

Chapter 9

THE PROPHETIC CAN RELEASE THE ANGELIC

THE WHO, WHAT, WHEN, AND WHERE OF ANGELS

1. Angels were created by God before He created the sun, earth, moon, and the rest of the universe.

2. They were in His presence as He created the universe. In fact, there was an angelic concert as God began to speak the universe into being. Perhaps they sang the "Hallelujah Chorus" or probably something even more awesome—whatever they sang created an environment of profound worship as God displayed His majestic power.

3. Angels, like you and me, have a free will; they are not slaves to God. We know this because the Bible says that about a third of the angelic host made the bad choice to leave Heaven and become God's enemy.

4. Unlike you and me, angels have supernatural knowledge and wisdom. Their superior understanding comes from living in the same spiritual realm God inhabits.

5. They have supernatural strength. We see it displayed many times throughout the Bible.

6. Angels have the ability to appear as humans. There are secret agent angels among us on short-term mission

assignments from Heaven. Hebrews 13:2 (NLT) confides: *"Don't forget to show hospitality to strangers, for some who have done this have entertained angels without realizing it!"*

7. Angels do not operate under the limitations of our physical world because they can transcend time, space, and matter.

8. They do not reproduce. Angels are incapable of procreation. Jesus tells us this in Matthew 22:30 (NLT): *"For when the dead rise, they will neither marry nor be given in marriage. In this respect they will be like the angels in heaven."*

9. Angels are never to be worshipped. Colossians 2:18 (NLT) says: *"Don't let anyone condemn you by insisting on pious self-denial or the worship of angels, saying they have had visions about these things...."*

In the New Age movement, there are people who worship fallen angels as "spiritual beings" yet deny the existence of their Creator, God. This is a great sin. Throughout Scripture angels have always commanded people not to worship them, rather they pointed their worship toward God.

Lucifer, Heaven's former choir director, was kicked out of Heaven because he coveted worship that was rightfully given only to God.

CATEGORIES OF ANGELS

According to Hebrews 12:22, angels are countless and all around us. There are three different kinds or classes of angels spoken of in the Bible, although there could be more types. The three mentioned are archangels, cherubim, and seraphim. Let's look at each more closely.

1. The first type are archangels. The angel Michael is a leader of angel armies and the only angel the Bible calls an archangel. Gabriel, who is described in Scripture as God's messenger, is believed to be an archangel also, but is never named as one. Lucifer may be an archangel, too. Both of the archangels we know of, Michael and Gabriel, don't have wings—they look like men.

2. Another class of angel is the cherubim. They are exotic and beautiful, have four wings, and are covered with

precious stones. Their job is to guard God's throne and His presence.

3. There are also angels called seraphim. Seraphim have six wings. They are described in Scripture as having two wings covering their face, two wings covering their feet, and the remaining two wings used for flight. Speaking to one another, they constantly declare the holiness of God.

ANGELS DON'T PREACH

Angels live under God's authority and they live by various rules. For example, because God was pleased with a Roman centurion named Cornelius, God sent an angel to him. The angel wasn't sent to preach the Good News of salvation to Cornelius; rather, he told Cornelius to contact Peter who could give him information about the Savior (Acts 10:22).

It is important to note that angels are not allowed to preach the Gospel, only humans are given that privilege.

If I were God, I would send beautiful angels to flutter their wings and hover ten feet off the ground to preach the Good News. Instead, due to God's unknowable wisdom, you get me and some other fortunate but equally unimpressive people to present the Gospel. I'm just guessing, but possibly God knew that beautiful, glorious angels, while able to draw a big crowd, would probably distract people from the message of salvation unlike we ordinary-looking humans.

If someone tells you that an angel gave them a special revelation, beware. And if what they say can't be found in God's Word, it is in error. God says in Psalm 138:2 that He has magnified His Word above His name. Hence, if someone claims to have received something from God that is not in "His Word," then we cannot give it credence. The reliability of God's Word exceeds all our experiences, angelic or otherwise. The Bible is the meat of our existence and the basis for our theology and spiritual beliefs.

A HOST OF ANGELS

Hebrews 12:22 tells us that there are countless thousands of angels. There are angels everywhere although they are rarely seen. There are angels who protect us, angels who gather when God's people worship Him, and angels busy doing God's will in ways we will never know.

One of the gifts of the Spirit is discerning of spirits. Those who have this gift can sense angelic or demonic activity. People have told me that they saw an angel while I was preaching, and that is a good thing.

The problem with angels arises when we overemphasize them and underemphasize God, Christ, and the Scripture. We can't allow angels to become our focus.

WILL AN ANGEL OBEY YOU?

Psalm 103:19 says, *"The Lord has established His throne in heaven, and His kingdom rules over all."* This Scripture tells us that God is the King over Heaven and everything in it including angels, and He rules over all the earth and everything in it. Hence, we can conclude that angels obey God.

Psalm 103:20: *"Bless the Lord, you His angels, who excel in strength, who do His word, heeding the voice of His word."* First, notice that angels have superior strength. Next notice, the Bible declares that angels *"do His [God's] word."* Finally notice that this verse tells us that angels heed or listen for God's orders. The key word in all this is the term *word*. Is it merely a coincidence that we learned in previous chapters that the prophetic is also about God's "words"?

Angels heed, act, and move when God gives voice to His will with words. Their ears are fine-tuned to God's voice. You might be thinking, *Well, that means they hear God when He talks in Heaven*, and that is true.

However, God not only speaks in Heaven but also on earth. So, angels also react when they hear His will spoken on earth...through people.

THUS SAITH THE LORD

More than 400 times the King James Version of the Bible recounts that Old Testament prophets spoke the words *"thus saith the Lord,"* and whatever they declared came to pass. Almost always angels conveyed God's words that were spoken through His prophets and were fulfilled.

If a prophet in the Old Covenant could speak God's will and have angels react, then how much more should born-again sons and daughters of God be able to speak prophetically what God is saying and have angels act in response?

If God's Word is living inside you and you are certain that you know His will concerning a matter...if that knowledge does not come from personal opinions or desires or outside influences but comes from divine revelation...if it is spoken by the direction of God at the correct moment in the proper place—it will change the atmosphere and release the angelic to fulfill His word.

God's Word has a voice and angels harken to that voice; and as a child of God, it is possible for you to be the voice of God on the earth.

CONDITION, EXCEPTIONS, STIPULATIONS

Remember the story in Chapter 6 of Joshua gazing down on the walled city of Jericho and discovering a general of God's angelic host standing beside him? You will recall that He asked the angel, "Are you for me or are you against me?" The angel's answer is important to our understanding of our ability to command angels. The angel's reply was, "Neither."

Angels are neither for you or against you; they are not subject to your words. They are only and always subject to God and to His words.

Our status as children of God does not give us the right to order angels around on a whim. Quoting Scripture isn't enough to make angels follow our commands. Angels only respond to a *rhema* word from God.

THE *RHEMA* REVELATION

Perhaps you already know that in the New Testament there are two Greek words used to identify the words spoken by God—*logos* and *rhema*. *Logos* is the *written* word of God. *Rhema* is the *spoken* word of God. A *rhema* word is an understanding that God by the Holy Spirit quickens or energizes us at a specific time for a specific purpose.

The *logos* or the Bible is a compilation of all God's thoughts, the roadmap for humankind, and it is perfect in every way. The Word of God in written *logos* form is the book we call the Bible. You could say that the *logos* word speaks to your mind and produces a *knowing;* and a rhema word speaks to your heart and produces a *revelation.*

When the Holy Spirit gives you a *rhema* word, whether it is a verse of Scripture you read or words that you heard preached, something comes alive inside you.

It is through a *rhema* revelation that God awakens something inside of us to create a deposit of understanding that has the power to change our world. (You should probably read that sentence again.)

Our moment of revelation awakens our faith and that moment of revelation is proof that God wants you to have what He has shown you through words.

God never shows you what He does not want to give you. So when revelation comes and your faith is awakened, God is saying that you can have whatever it might be.

When something from God comes alive within you, it becomes your personal *rhema*. The way you activate that word into the natural world is by speaking it. Speaking back to God what you heard Him say is dynamic and becomes supernatural.

When you speak the *rhema* word out loud, angels hear the sound of God's voice in it. They harken to it because it was not born out of your mind but out of the mind of God. All you've done is given voice to what God revealed to you. Angels recognize God's voice spoken by any person anywhere in the world and they respond. When you begin to declare in prayer, in confession, or in worship God's word to you, you become

God's voice on the earth. Your act of verbalizing a word releases the power of God and the armies of Heaven to act upon your words.

What occurs to fulfill that *rhema* word is most often unseen and many times accomplished through God's workforce on earth—angels.

THE ANGEL OF KAMPALA, UGANDA

Several years ago, I was preaching in Uganda to four or five thousand pastors in a conference held at their Parliament building. I was speaking about the Joshua Generation and brought copies of my book on that subject to give to the pastors. While preaching, I started talking about angels who preside over cities.

At this meeting, I was ministering alongside a group of four pastors from Australia who were seated in the front row as I spoke that evening. When I started talking about angels who are in authority over cities, they dropped their Bibles, turned their heads up, their eyes widened, and their mouths dropped open. I figured that something unusual was happening to them.

I thought there must be a bat or bird flying close to the ceiling. Also, the power went off and on two or three times while I was speaking. After the service, the Australians came running up to me and said, "Pastor Maiden, Pastor Maiden, did you see it?"

"Did I see what?" I asked.

"The moment you said the angel of the Lord has been sent to cities, a giant being walked through the auditorium. He must have been 50 feet tall. In fact, he was so tall that it took only one step for him to pass all the way through the building."

It is interesting that all four men saw the same thing, as it is unusual for several people to have the same vision at the same time.

Remember again when Joshua was on that hill overlooking Jericho and met the angel. God had a plan to win at Jericho; because He won that city, He can win your city, too.

TO UNLOCK THE SUPERNATURAL, USE YOUR KEY

It is wrong to think that God in Heaven merely hands out marching orders to His angels every day. He does do that, but because there is an interaction between Heaven and earth, sometimes angels get their orders this side of Heaven, too.

Things we do on earth can release a spiritual reaction in the heavenly realm.

An example of this interaction between earth and Heaven is found in Psalm 22:3 (NLT): *"Yet you are holy, enthroned on the praises of Israel."* God inhabits the praises of His people; and when God establishes a presence somewhere on earth, it is always surrounded with angels. Hence, we know that anytime the spirit of God is moving, there is always a presence of angels.

When we command a demon to leave in Jesus' name, the demon hears the command as if Jesus is standing before him. When we command a disease to leave someone in Jesus' name, the disease hears the command as if Jesus said it. I'm not Jesus and neither are you, but we have been given His name to use on the earth.

Jesus said: *"And I will give you the keys of the kingdom of heaven, and whatever you bind on earth will be bound in heaven, and whatever you loose on earth will be loosed in heaven"* (Matthew 16:19).

Everything God ever revealed to you became a "key" capable of binding and loosening. Every promise in Scripture…every understanding of what God has done for you in Christ…every time you received a *rhema* word…every time you received an insight from God, you received a key that works on Heaven and earth.

Now it is up to you whether or not you use that key to change your world. What will you do?

Just prior to Jesus' promise of giving the keys, Peter had declared his *rhema* word that Jesus was the Messiah, the Son of God:

> *Jesus replied, "You are blessed, Simon son of John, because* **my Father in heaven has**

> **revealed this to you.** *You did not learn this from any human being. Now I say to you that you are Peter (which means 'rock'), and* **upon this rock I will build my church,** *and all the powers of hell will not conquer it"* (Matthew 16:17-18 NLT).

Jesus was telling Peter that he was blessed because he received a revelation and spoke it, and that had changed him.

Becoming a child of God didn't just give you a superior title or change your relationship with God, it also changed your spiritual abilities and authority because now you have *"the keys."*

Revelation Is Ownership

It is time for the Church and we who as a are the Church to move from the place of harboring revelation and storing up truth to declaring it, expressing it, and living it out. To put it another way, it is time to use your keys! Your keys will stop the devil and your keys will open Heaven.

When you have a need, don't beg God for help, use your key. Several years ago, while praying I was begging God for money. I said, "You know my heart's good. You know how generous we are. You know I'm a giver." Yes, I was trying to butter Him up. Then it seemed like God was right there with me and replied to my prayer in a firm, loud voice, "Stop begging Me for money!"

That was not the revelation I was hoping for during my prayer time.

Then He lowered His tone and said to me, "Tell the enemy to let go of your money." When I was younger, I would do that all the time, but I'd been through some difficult times and my faith was diminished. Anything you need you have the authority to loose if you have a word about it.

THE LANGUAGE OF ANGELS?

First Corinthians 13:1 says, *"Though I speak with the tongues of men and of angels, but have not love, I have become sounding brass or a clanging cymbal."*

It is interesting that the most famous chapter on love is sandwiched between two chapters that speak about spiritual gifts. I think the location is not coincidental because I've known people who had powerful spiritual gifts, yet whose effectiveness was diminished by their lack of love.

First Corinthians 13:1 reminds me of another found in Romans 8:26: *"Likewise the Spirit also helps in our weaknesses. For we do not know what we should pray for as we ought...."* This verse tells us that we have a narrow understanding and a limited view of what is going on and therefore often don't know the best way to pray for it. Yet the Holy Spirit will help us pray in the right way.

Our weakness is a lack of understanding; but the strength of the Holy Spirit, who resides in us, is His omniscience, He completely understands.

The verse in Romans goes on to say that the Holy Spirit makes up for our weakness in a very interesting way: *"...the Spirit Himself makes intercession for us with groanings which cannot be uttered"* (Romans 8:26). Obviously these groanings of the Spirit cannot be expressed in a human language. I believe "groaning" is talking about words that are not part of any language.

Even though the words used by the Holy Spirit are not from a language we know, they are from a language understood by Christ: *"Now He who searches the hearts knows what the mind of the Spirit is, because He makes intercession for the saints according to the will of God"* (Romans 8:27).

BENEFITS OF PRAYING IN TONGUES

I believe there are three primary benefits that manifest when we pray in tongues:

1. **Personal Edification.** According to First Corinthians 14:4, praying in tongues strengthens us. So, I pray in tongues as often as possible.

2. **Deeper Worship.** After praying everything I can think of, I move to a

higher plane and allow my spirit to enter the inexhaustible realm of worship found in heavenly tongues.

3. **Accurate Intercession.** According to Romans 8:26, we can allow the Holy Spirit within us to take over and pray through us the exact mind and will of God.

We learned earlier in the chapter that when we speak God's will, angels respond to implement it. So let me ask you, could praying in tongues be the language of angels that is spoken of in First Corinthians 13:1, as some believe?

PHONE CALL TO AN ANGEL

As a 19-year-old Bible college student, I had a part-time job in downtown Los Angeles. During my lunch break one day, I was talking on the phone to my sweetheart, Mary. She was the church secretary at my father's church. This was "BC," before cellphones, so I was talking on a pay phone. As a lovesick 19-year-old, I was putting in quarter after quarter to stay on the line. In the middle of our conversation, she said that she had to put me on hold because someone had entered the office.

As soon as she said that, the Holy Spirit gave me the impression that she was in danger. That was all I got, in danger, which was obviously not enough to call the police. (Did I mention that the church was across the street from a mental hospital?)

I didn't know what to do. So I fell on my knees in that phone booth and began groaning in "other tongues." I didn't know what the situation was so I didn't know how to pray, but the Holy Spirit within me knew the perfect prayer.

I continued to pump quarters into the payphone to stay on the line even though I was on hold. It must have been about five minutes later when she finally came back on the phone crying and terrified. A man had walked into the office holding a knife and bleeding. He looked at her, came right up to her, and asked her if she was alone and she was. I knew that while I was groaning in the Spirit, angels were being released to protect her. She came through that possibly fatal situation unharmed.

JESUS TALKS ABOUT ANGELS

In Matthew 26, when the priests and their armed men came to take Jesus into custody, Peter drew his sword to protect Jesus and cut off a man's ear. You may know the story; Jesus reattached the guy's ear. Then He turned to Peter and said, *"Don't you realize that I could ask my Father for thousands of angels to protect us, and he would send them instantly?"* (Matthew 26:53 NLT).

I want you to notice that Jesus didn't tell Peter that He, Jesus, could have called down angels. I mention this because I know there are ministries that claim to command angels, but that belief is not supported by Scripture.

Nevertheless, in this chapter we have learned that we do have the ability to release supernatural power, which may include activating angels.

ACTS OF ANGELS IN THE EARLY CHURCH

Throughout the book of Acts there are many manifestations of angels. One of the first such incidences was when an angel freed Peter after the demonized King Herod put him in jail. This angelic act happened while intercession for Peter was going on at John Mark's house. The Church had no military power or political power, but they did have Kingdom power. It is obvious that their prayers for Peter's deliverance released the angelic to deliver him.

What they did not do is send angels; rather, they were talking to God, interceding and speaking God's word of deliverance for Peter. Then God sent the angel.

The angel came to Peter, woke him up, told him to get dressed and follow him. God had already said that Peter would die a very old man. In John 21:18 (NLT), Jesus told Peter, *"...when you are old, you will stretch out your hands, and others will dress you and take you where you don't want to go."*

That means that Peter was not destined to die by the hand of Herod at this early moment in church history. Not only did the prayers of those early Christians release their pastor from prison, but their prayers also brought down Herod's government in the same month. Not long after Peter's escape from jail, Herod was struck down by an angel because he accepted for himself glory that belonged to God.

Later, an angel directed Philip to share the Gospel with an Ethiopian eunuch of great authority.

> *As for Philip, an angel of the Lord said to him, "Go south down the desert road that runs from Jerusalem to Gaza." So he started out, and he met the treasurer of Ethiopia, a eunuch of great authority under the Kandake, the queen of Ethiopia...* (Acts 8:26-27 NLT).

You will notice that the angel didn't tell him what to say but put him on the right road and suggested that he make himself available to be a witness for Christ.

Based on the accounts of angels in the New Testament, I believe that angels are not allowed to give the Church doctrinal instruction either directly or indirectly through someone else.

DO YOU HAVE A GUARDIAN ANGEL?

The answer is, "No, not exactly…you have something better." You may have noticed that guardian angels were not among the categories of angels mentioned earlier in this chapter. In fact, the term "guardian angels" cannot be found in the Bible; however, you have scores of angels watching over you! The following are a few Scriptures that mention your angelic bodyguards:

> *If you make the Lord your refuge, if you make the Most High your shelter, no evil will conquer you; no plague will come near your home.* **For he will order his angels to protect you wherever you go. They will hold you up with their hands** *so you won't even hurt your foot on a stone* (Psalm 91:9-12 NLT).

> *The angel of the Lord encamps all around those who fear Him, and delivers them* (Psalm 34:7).

The term used in the second Scripture, *"encamps around,"* means angels are protecting you from attacks coming from every direction. When King David went to war, his tent was set up in the very middle of the camp. For enemies to reach him, they would have to go through as many as twenty layers of soldiers. God is saying to you, "I've got you covered. There are layers of angels surrounding you." I like that better than a guardian angel.

I believe the-last days Church will see the most angelic activity in all of history. Hell has opened and is releasing everything it has to defeat the Church at this crucial time—but Heaven is releasing an even greater grace. That *greater grace* has a purpose and we who are called by His name are being given more power and authority than ever before to overcome evil and fill the earth with the glory of God.

AN ANGEL ALERT

Although angels are superior to humankind in almost every way, in eternity, when we have become all that God created us to be and Jesus died for us to become, you and I will judge the angels. So regardless of the supernatural things that may go on around us, both good and evil, we can't allow ourselves to be distracted from the job we have been given.

Angels, as majestic as they are, are merely a method God uses to implement His will; so we must keep our focus on the One who created the angels rather than on His creation. We must not fall prey to one of the devil's strategies to make Christians and the Church ineffec- tual: the distraction provided by the manifestation of supernatural beings. Distracting us from Jesus and our purpose is one of his most effective ploys. He would scare us with demons or astonish us with angels.

However, we refuse to be frightened by demons or awed by angels; we have a higher place than either of them in God's plans—we are the redeemed, the children of the Most High God!

ABOUT DR. MICHAEL MAIDEN

Dr. Michael Maiden and Mary, his beloved wife of more than 40 years, are the senior pastors of Church for the Nations in Phoenix, Arizona. Here he strongly and lovingly prepares God's people for service in God's Kingdom. The messages are always relevant, timely, and life changing as well as prophetic.

Dr. Maiden earned a Master's and a Doctorate degree in Christian Psychology. He has authored seven books including *The Joshua Generation: God's Manifesto for the End Time Church* and *Turn the World Upside Down,* which addresses how to maximize the impact of God-given gifts by identifying the seven major mountains of influence established in society.

In addition to his work in the local church, he is a strong prophetic voice to every generation and has ministered to public officials as well as pastors and ministers around the world. Dr. Maiden is president and CEO of Church on the Rock International, a dynamic ministry that oversees more than 6,000 churches worldwide. He is also on the board of Fishers of Men International, the Jewish Voice International, and several local churches.